GW01373438

British Battlefields Series

The Right Worshipfull S.r William Balfour late Leutenent of the Tower of London etc: and now Collonell of A Regi.mt under the Earle of Essex

The most noble and truly Valiant S.r Bevill Granville of Stowe in the County of Cornwall

Civil War Battles in Cornwall
1642 to 1646

Richard Holmes

Civil War Battles in Cornwall 1642-1646
First published in August 1989 by Mercia Publications Ltd, The Science Park,
University of Keele, Staffordshire ST5 5SP

Copyright: Mercia Publications Ltd.

No part of this book may be reproduced by whatever means without the written permission of the publishers.

ISBN 0 948087 32 3

Printed by J H Brookes (Printers) Ltd, 141-149 Lower Bryan Street, Hanley, Stoke-on-Trent ST1 5AX

CONTENTS

		Page
1:	The Coming of Civil War	5
2:	Opening Rounds, 1642-43	20
3:	Triumph and Tragedy: The Cornish Abroad, 1643	36
4:	The Lostwithiel Campaign 1644	49
5:	The End in the West, 1645-46	65
	Epilogue	74
	Notes	80

ACKNOWLEDGMENTS

We gratefully acknowledge permission to reproduce portraits as follows:
National Portrait Gallery: Charles 1, the Earl of Essex, Lord Hopton, Sir Bevil Grenvile, and Sir William Balfour.
The Courtauld Institute of Art: The Earl of Stamford.
The County Museum, Truro: Anthony Payne.

All photographs were taken by the author.
Maps by Elizabeth Saxton.

1. THE COMING OF CIVIL WAR

i. The Land and the People

Even in the late 20th Century Cornwall is set apart from the remainder of Britain. Modern civil engineering has mitigated the physical obstacles confronting the outsider, but the bastions on Cornwall's borders—Plymouth and Okehampton—still impose delay. Harsh Dartmoor and gentler Exmoor form a glacis on the Devon side of the Tamar, and the river remains a psychological frontier even if it is more easily crossed by motor car than by the pack-horse or mail-coach of yesteryear. The bleak expanse of Bodmin Moor dominates the eastern end of the county. The rivers Fowey, Camel and Fal slash inland, restricting East-West movement even in an age which takes bridges for granted.

The coastline, rocky and inhospitable, is broken by the estuaries of its three main rivers and by the transverse gash of the Helford River. The seaports of Falmouth, Fowey and Padstow—only the former now retaining anything approaching its former status—shelter in the estuaries, and scores of fishing villages, now magnets for tourists, nestle in clefts in the coast. This rough land is buffeted by hard weather. The Cornish microclimate remains the peril of holidaymakers and fishermen alike: there is more than a little truth in the saying that it rains once a day and twice on Sundays. The sea is never far away: as A. L. Rowse wrote, "its scent and rumour is everywhere."[1]

A hard land breeds self-reliant people. Part of the Cornish character stems from the county's remoteness and from the difficulty of ploughing a living from the soil or hauling it from the sea. Nor was that other Cornish occupation, mining, any easier. There were tinners in Cornwall long before the Romans came, and in the Middle Ages a succession of Charters for the Stannaries established the status of the tinners themselves, their Stannary Courts and the four Stannary towns—Helston, Truro, Lostwithiel and Liskeard. Tin was "streamed" from river banks until the mid 15th Century, when mining became the norm, its underground drudgery made dangerous by flooding, cave-ins and foul air.

But there is more to the Cornish character than the natural strength created by

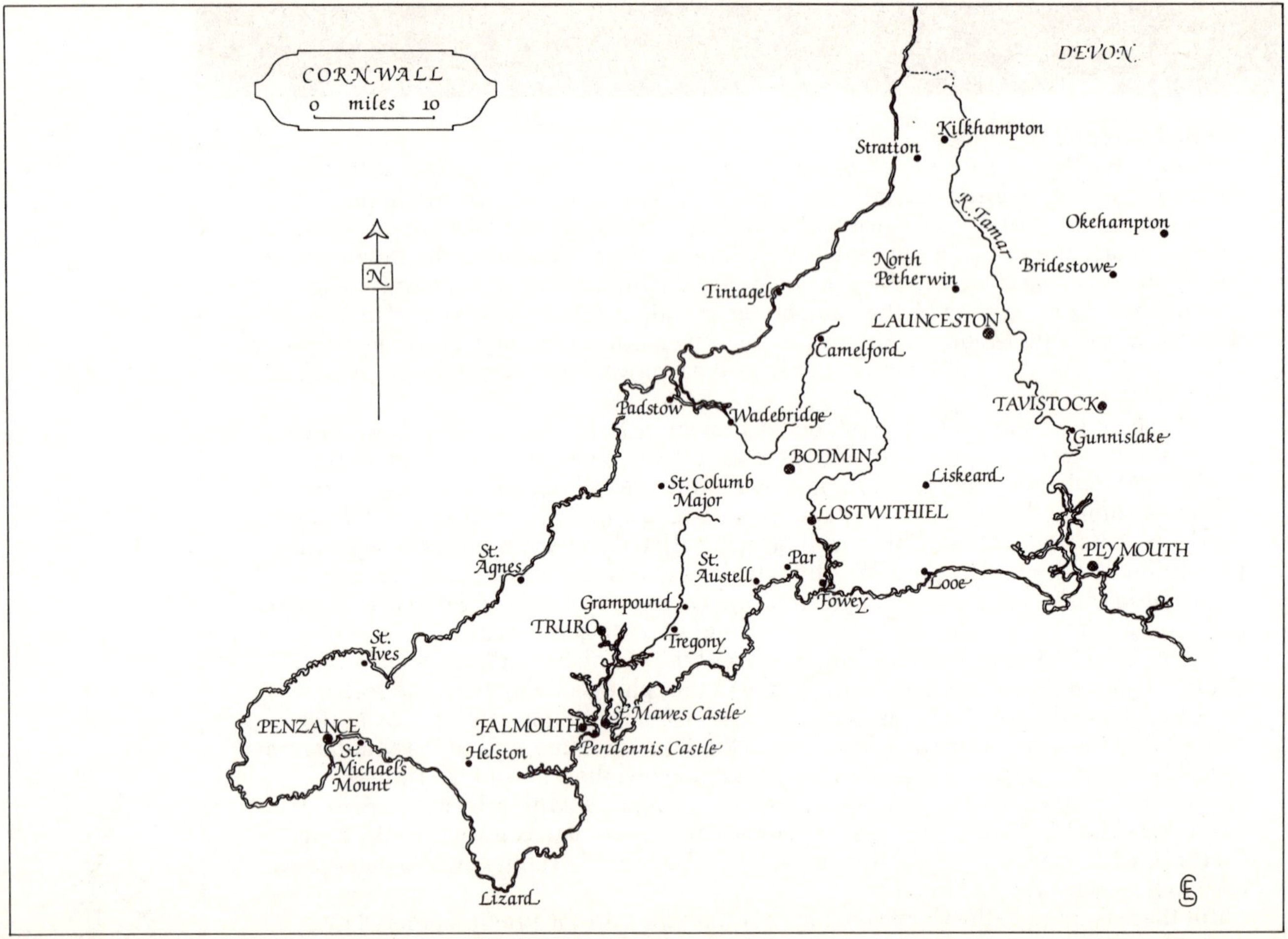

CORNWALL
0 miles 10
N
DEVON
Kilkhampton
Stratton
R. Tamar
Okehampton
North Petherwin
Bridestowe
Tintagel
LAUNCESTON
Camelford
TAVISTOCK
Padstow
Wadebridge
Gunnislake
BODMIN
St. Columb Major
Liskeard
LOSTWITHIEL
St. Agnes
St. Austell
Par
PLYMOUTH
Looe
Grampound
Fowey
TRURO
Tregony
St. Ives
St. Mawes Castle
PENZANCE
FALMOUTH
St. Michael's Mount
Helston
Pendennis Castle
Lizard

pushing hard against a robust environment. The precise recipe for the geneological cocktail making up the Cornishman must remain a matter of conjecture, but Cretan traders and shipwrecked Armada mariners may have made their contribution, adding an almost Mediterranean flair to a dogged and resolute personality. Though the overland connections between Cornwall and the rest of Britain were at times tenuous, the sheer variety of seaborne trade is remarkable. Excavations at Tintagel Castle have disclosed oil jars from Tunisia, dishes from Carthage and Asia Minor, wine amphoras from the Greek Islands or Turkey, jars from near the modern Instanbul.[2] Celtic place-names are survivals of the language that was widely spoken until Tudor times, a Celtic dialect more akin to Breton than Welsh: its conscious revival is marked by the use of the Celtic *Kernow* for Cornwall. When the Venetian ambassador found himself marooned in Falmouth by bad weather in 1506, he complained that his hosts were "so different in language and custom from the Londoners and the rest of England that they are as unintelligible to these last as to the Venetians."[3]

Undercurrents of superstition run deep. Granite tombs and monuments, earthen barrows and concentric forts, march across the landscape. Evidence of more recent beliefs is furnished by the sturdy, self-confident churches, so many of them rebuilt in the late 15th Century before the hard edge of the Reformation pruned ornate excesses. Methodist chapels testify to the colossal impact of John Wesley, who first visited the county in 1743 and converted the hard-living tinners in their thousands.

The great houses of Cornwall are as distinctive a feature of the Cornish landscape as church or chapel. The connection between the church and the great house is no accident, for many were built around former priories or on land once owned by the monastries dissolved by Henry VIII. The disposal of monastic lands following the dissolution of the monasteries strengthened the position of those families who could afford to buy them, setting the seal on fortunes made in mining, trade or the sort of maritime adventuring which sometimes looked much like piracy. The Rashleighs, a family of successful merchants, bought Bodmin priory, but did not live there, building instead at Menabilly, in a splended setting between Tywardreath and Fowey, and the Grenviles, Godolphins, Prideaux and Arundells were all well to the fore in the scramble for land. The Robartes of Truro made their fortune in tin and seized the opportunity to obtain land by purchasing the monastic farm at Lanhydrock, and went on to gain ennoblement and build the finest Jacobean house in the country.[4]

The Arundells lived in Lanherne by St Mawgan, and John Arundell built Trerice, south-east of Newquay, its gables in the Dutch style perhaps reflecting the influence of his time spent soldiering in the Low Countries. The Godolphins of Godolphin Hall grew rich from the tin-mines in their land, and the Bassetts of Tehidy and St Michael's Mount also made their fortunes from it. Cothele, which Rowse rightly calls the most beautiful of Cornish houses, lies above the Tamar, where Sir Richard Edgcumbe, friend of Henry VII, built it, and Mount Edgecumbe itself still stands squarely across the estuary from Plymouth.

The independence of the Cornish was brusquely demonstrated long before the Dissolution. In 1497 there was widespread resistance to a subsidy levied to pay for Henry VII's Scottish war. The rebels were led by Michael Joseph, a blacksmith from St Keverne, and Richard Flamank, a lawyer from Bodmin. The gentry held aloof, although James, Lord Audley, joined the rebels in Wells. The Cornishmen marched on London, and mid-June saw them on Blackheath, where the royal forces cut them to pieces. Joseph and Flamank suffered the barbarous penalty of hanging, drawing and quartering: Audley's nobility brought him the more merciful axe. Scarcely was Audley's head off his shoulders than the West was stirring again: Perkin Warbeck, pretender to the throne, landed at Whitsand Bay near Land's End in September 1497, and attracted a substantial following. Perkin's little army disintegrated when it failed to take Exeter. Few of the rebels were executed, but Henry, with a Tudor's eye to the coffers, confiscated the land of rebel supporters and levied widespread fines, impoverishing much of the county and deepening its feeling of separateness.

If the gentry had avoided involvement in the rebellions of 1497, their loyalties were more sorely tried in 1549 when the Cornish rose against the imposition of a new prayer-book. Humphry Arundell and John Winsdale, both well-to-do-men, led them. They took Plymouth and laid siege to Exeter, where they were defeated with much slaughter by Lords Russell and Grey. Numerous priests paid the supreme penalty for their involvement with the rebels: the vicar of St Thomas's Exeter was hanged in chains from his own church-tower, in an affirmation of Protestant supremacy which would not be forgotten a century later. The Arundells suffered severely: both Humphry and his cousin Sir Thomas were executed, and thereafter the family remained obdurately devoted to the old religion, and became the mainstay of catholicism in Cornwall.

ii. The Military Background

Tudor Cornishmen displayed as much valour in foreign war as they did in resistance to the distant authority of London. The Cornish coast had long been subject to French and Spanish raids, and when the activities of English privateers, so many of them West Country men, seemed likely to provoke Spanish reprisals, steps were taken to reinforce the area's defences. Henry VII had diverted some of the money and material from the Dissolution of the Monastries to the construction of castles and blockhouses along the coast from Hull to Milford Haven, and the castles of St Mawes and Pendennis were built at the mouth of the Fal, securing the entrance to Falmouth harbour. Their captains, frequently in trouble because of their questionable associations with pirates and privateering activities on their own account, usually came from the most solid Cornish families: Killigrew, Treffry and Arundell amongst them. Late in Elizabeth's reign Henry's great drum towers were reinforced by bastioned earthworks, a muster was taken of the county militia, weapons were sent down to the West, and private arsenals were surveyed. John Treffry had enough equipment for two dozen well-armed men, and well he might, for his house in Fowey had been the target for French raiders on at least one occasion.

Cornwall 1642

The defence of the realm in Tudor and Stuart times was the responsibility of county militias. Forces for foreign expeditions, like Elizabeth's Irish wars or the abortive Isle de Rhé expedition of 1627, were raised by calling for volunteers, who were usually supplemented with pressed men. Barnaby Rich wrote in 1587 that "when service happens we disburthen the prisons of thieves, we rob the taverns and alehouses of tosspots and ruffians, we scour both town and country of rogues and vagabonds."[5] All Englishmen were liable for service in the militia: a man's income determined whether he provided an armed horseman or served on foot. Elizabethan legislation fined down this general levy by directing that each county should select "a convenient number of able men" who could be trained at the county's expense—the origin of the expression "trained bands." At the time of the Armada perhaps 130,000 men could be brought together under arms, and 160,000 were said to be available in 1623.[6]

Two points about the militia are of special relevance to the story that follows. The first is that Cornwall was militarily more important, because of the Spanish threat, than many other counties, and the arming of the militia was taken more seriously than it was elsewhere. In 1580, 4,000 men were selected for militia service: 2,000 were to march into Devon if required, and three companies of 100 each were to garrison St Mawes, Pendennis and St Michael's Mount. Men were to be trained ten times a year by captains who moved from one group of three parishes to the next. Sir Richard Grenvile—mortally wounded aboard *Revenge* in a fight against impossible odds in 1591—was the senior of the county's four generals. Secondly, in Cornwall as elsewhere the militia was controlled by local magnates, the lord-lieutenant and his deputies. In 1586, for instance, Sir Walter Raleigh was lord lieutenant, with Sir William Mohun and Sir Francis Godolphin as his deputies, and in the following autumn these worthies had 5,560 armed men under their command. The central authority in London relied upon its local representatives to summon the militia: the defection of key magnates, or the inability of their hastily-appointed replacements to enforce their will, were to have important consequences when the Civil War broke out.

Although there was no standing army in Tudor and Stuart England, there was a sprinkling of men with military experience. Some had fought the Spaniards on the continent in Elizabeth's time; others had taken part in expeditions to France or Germany during the reigns of James I or Charles I, or served in European armies during the Thirty Years War. Such men were highly sought-after in the early stages of the Civil War, for their professional knowledge provided an invaluable leavening to the largely amateur armies that fought for King and Parliament alike. Even the principal infantry weapons of the Civil War, the musket and the pike, were not easily managed, and the contribution made by experienced soldiers to the raising and training of both armies can scarcely be over-emphasised.

The expression "both armies" is itself an oversimplification, for until the formation of Parliament's New Model Army in 1645 each of the contending parties in the Civil War had not one army, but several. While the King's main army was based on his capital of Oxford, the Marquis of Newcastle maintained a large army in the north-east, and there were substantial local forces elsewhere. Similarly, although Parliament's main army was based upon London, local associations had large forces of their own. Nevertheless, the command structures of the opposing forces looked remarkably similar. In overall command was a captain-general, with a lieutenant-general as his second in command. Each of the major arms—horse, foot and artillery—had its own general and lieutenant-general. The foot also had a sergeant-major-general (soon abbreviated to major-general), while the commissary-general carried out a similar function in the cavalry.[7] Some senior officers were chosen for their social standing rather than their military efficiency, and it was usual to provide these gentlemen with a second-in-command who knew his business. Command was more diluted than it is today, for decisions off the field of battle were usually taken by a council of war consisting of an army's senior officers.

Infantry formed the bulk of Civil War armies. The proportion of pikemen in the infantry had fallen steadily, and by the outbreak of war perhaps two-thirds of infantry were musketeers: the New Model was certainly raised on this basis. The pikeman's main weapon, the pike, was a regulation length of 18 feet, although in practice it was much shorter, for soldiers were given to cutting their weapons down to make them less cumbersome on the march. In Elizabeth's time the pikemen had worn breast- and backplate, the morion-like helmet known as a "pikeman's pot", a gorget at his throat and long articulated tassets covering his thighs. By the Civil War gorget and tassets had been abandoned, and as the war went on the corslet itself was often discarded. The pikeman also wore a sword, but there were repeated complaints that this weapon was often misused to cut up firewood or to trim branches to make huts.

Although the musketeer was spared the burden of body armour, he carried a cumbersome musket, its barrel four feet long, firing a bullet weighing one twelfth of a pound. A rest, forked at one end and pointed at the other, was used to support the musket in firing. It was loaded by tipping a charge of powder down the barrel, following this with a ball, and ramming wadding—tow, paper or grass—after it. The musketeer usually carried twelve ready-made charges in tubular containers hung from a leather shoulder belt called the bandolier, and in battle he would keep a number of bullets in his mouth to save fumbling for them in his pouch. Having loaded his weapon, the musketeer primed it, putting fine priming powder from his flask into the musket's pan. The weapon was fired by a piece of smouldering cord, known as the match, which was gripped in the jaws of the cock: pressing the trigger brought the match down into the priming pan, igniting the powder there and firing the piece. Loading and firing a matchlock musket was a complicated business, and was taught in a number of drill movements. Momentary inattention or panic could result in a misfire or, worse still, in the premature explosion of the charge or of the prepared charges in the bandolier. Even the most accomplished musketeer would find his task impeded by wind and rain, and the need to have lighted matches made night operations difficult to conceal. Match disappeared at an alarming rate: the garrison of Lyme, 1,500 strong, often used five hundredweight in 24 hours. The musket was effective at 400 yards, but its real fighting range was probably a good deal less, perhaps 150 yards, dwindling further as powder-smoke reduced visibility.

Armour was in decline amongst the cavalry just as it was in the infantry. Although a few cavalry units wore full armour—Sir Arthur Hesilrig's "lobsters" were the most famous—senior commanders were often portrayed clad in armour. Most officers and troopers wore breast- and backplate and a lobster-tailed helmet with a triple-barred face-guard or single sliding nasal. The buff coat, a stout leather garment, often with sleeves, was worn under—or instead of—the cuirass. A broad-brimmed felt hat, sometimes reinforced with a steel "spider" inside the crown was a popular alternative to the helmet: it is certainly not the case that all Royalists wore felt hats and all Roundheads the lobstertail.

The cavalryman carried a long, straight sword with a basket hilt, a pair of wheel-lock pistols—their charges ignited by a toothed wheel revolving against a piece of iron pyrites held in the jaws of the cock—and, on occasion, a carbine. The Civil War came at a time when cavalry tactics were the subject of controversy. Officers brought up in the "Dutch school" argued in favour of trotting up to within pistol range of the enemy, whence each rank would fire its pistols and move to the regiment's rear to reload. Advocates of the "Swedish school" maintained that cavalry should achieve its result by the shock action of man and horse, not by the fire of its pistols: they favoured charging home, and not firing a shot till they were in the enemy's ranks. The war saw the complete victory of the Swedish school, and the most successful cavalry leaders on both sides emphasised the importance of momentum and vigour in the charge.

The dragoon was a hybrid. Although he was mounted, his steed was of poorer quality than the cavalryman's. He had no defensive armour, wore a cloth rather than a buff-coat, and carried both sword and musket. The dragoon generally dismounted to fight on foot, although the New Model's dragoons followed up their fire by a mounted charge at Naseby. In the advance, dragoons moved with the vanguard to hold key features or defiles until the infantry came up, and in retreat they held ground to cover the army's retirement. They were well suited to carrying out all sorts of outpost work, and in battle they were often used to line hedges on an army's flanks.

Artillery, which was to become the greatest casualty-producer on the 20th Century battlefield, was in its infancy in the 17th Century. The practice of attaching light guns to regiments of foot had been widely followed on the continent during the Thirty Years War, and was continued in the Civil War. There was no real standardisation of the weight or calibre of artillery at the time of the Civil War. However, it progressed from the tiny robinet, firing a 3/4 pound ball, through the falconet, falcon, minion, saker, demi-culverin, culverin, demi-cannon, and cannon, to the cannon royal with its 63-pound ball. The weight of the larger guns made them more suitable for seige or fortress duty than for service with a field army, and 5-pounder sakers and 9-pounder demi-culverins were the most common types of field gun. The culverin, more rarely seen in the field, threw its 15-pound shot a maximum of 2,650 yards, and needed a team of eight horses to pull it. Bad roads and inclement weather, the rule rather than the exception in Civil War Cornwall, made for extra horses, bogged guns, and much unparliamentary language amongst the train of artillery.

An army's train would number anything from ten or fifteen guns to as many as fifty. The Earl of Essex, Parliamentarian commander in the Lostwithiel campaign of 1644, lost all his "49 pieces of fair brass ordnance" including "the great Basilisco of Dover." We must admire the efforts of Sir John Merrick, Essex's general of the ordnance, in hauling such an unwieldy beast so far: if it was indeed a basiliske, it would have required something like fourteen yoke of oxen or twenty horses to draw it.

Despite the affection of modern film-makers for depicting exploding shells in 17th Century battles, only mortars, whose use was generally confined to static operations, actually fired such missiles, and then with much uncertainty. The solid roundshot was the main projectile of field artillery, although case-shot—a canister of musket balls which spread in a wide arc on leaving the muzzle—could be fired at close range, and was frequently used by "regimental pieces" in the infantry. Each gun was manned by the gunner, his mate, and a number of labourers or matrosses.[8]

The regiment, named after its colonel, was the standard unit of organisation in both horse and foot in both sides in the Civil War. A regiment's establishment varied. The New Model's regiments of foot had 1,200 men, divided into ten companies. The colonel's company, commanded by his captain-lieutenant, was 200 strong, the lieutenant-colonel's 160 and the major's 140: the other companies, captain's commands, numbered 100 apiece. In practice, regiments were often much smaller than their establishments suggested, and regiments with 2-300 men under arms were not uncommon. Each company had its own colour, carried by the ensign, the most junior of its three officers. Cavalry troops—the equivalent of companies—had a standard each, and dragoon companies bore a guidon. Regiments of horse or foot were often brigaded together under a general officer or the senior colonel.

Logisticians are the cinderellas of military history, whose undramatic but trojan efforts so often pass unnoticed. It is only when the commissariat fails or transport breaks down that they attract attention.[9] Soldiers were entitled to a daily ration, or cash instead. Sir James Turner, an officer of wide experience in Britain and on the continent, wrote of how:

> they allow so much bread, flesh, wine or beer to every trooper and foot soldier, which is ordinarily alike to both, then they allow to the officers, according to their dignities and charges, double, triple and quadruple portions; as to an ensign four times more than to a common soldier, a colonel commonly having twelve portions allowed him. The ordinary allowance for a soldier in the field is daily, two pound of bread, one pound of flesh, or in lieu of it, one pound of cheese, one pottle of wine, or in lieu of it, two pottles of beer.[10]

Turner had certainly identified the most common items in the Civil War soldier's diet—bread and cheese. But as he admitted, there was sometimes little connection between theory and practice, because food was simply not available. A 17th Century army lived largely off the country it passed through, although its baggage train would generally contain enough provisions to meet temporary shortfalls. Campaigning in a thinly-populated area, or one which had recently been gnawed bare by passing armies, meant empty bellies and worsening discipline. One expedient was to resort to "free quarter" by billeting soldiers on households over a wide area. The soldiers' hosts were paid a daily allowance, but this took the form of a debenture which had to be cashed by some responsible authority, and difficulties often arose. Free quarter had the dual disadvantage of impeding the army's concentration in the event of surprise, and drastically worsening relations with civilians. Requisitioning provisions, again on promise of eventual payment, also provoked resentment.

A commander who tried to make his army self-sufficient would lengthen his baggage train, and thus reduce his operational mobility: in 1606 the Spanish general Spinola had no less than 2,000 waggons for just 15,000 soldiers. The growing needs of the artillery lengthened an army's logistic tail. When the Royalist train of artillery was packed ready to move at Oxford in October 1642 it formed three great divisions of wheeled transport, and in 1647 the New Model's artillery and baggage-train required 1,038 horses. Horses, naturally enough, required feeding, and the need to provide fodder imposed yet another logistic burden. Supply and transport were the responsibility of different officers. The "commissary for the provisions" or "general proviant-master" supervised the commissariat, while the "carriage-master-general" or "baggage-master-general" had the unenviable task of controlling the transport.

The state of Cornwall's roads cannot have pleased the baggage-masters of either army. The roads of Britain were not properly mapped until the first volume of John Ogilby's magnificent *Britannia* appeared in 1675, but there had probably been little improvement since the 1640s. Cornwall was particularly ill-served. Three main routes ran into the county. The first, from Okehampton, crossed the Tamar at Polston Bridge below Launceston, and ran on to Camelford, Padstow and Truro. The second ran from Tavistock across the Tamar at Newbridge near Calstock, passing through Liskeard, Lostwithiel and Grampound on its way to Truro. The coast road from Plymouth ran on through Looe to Fowey, St Austell, Tregony, Penzance and Land's End. Smaller roads linked Launceston to Bodmin, Padstow to Stratton, and Lostwithiel to Fowey.[11] Roads were poorly maintained, and became treacherous in bad weather.

iii. The Outbreak of War

One of the major contributions to English historiography over the past half-century has been the immense amount of work done on the breakdown which plunged the country into war in 1642. Three main thrusts may be identified. One has been spearheaded by Ronald Hutton, whose work on the raising of the Royalist army has gone some way towards redressing the balance of historical writing, its scales heavily weighted by Christopher Hill and others, which portrayed the nation as generally Parliamentarian in its sympathies. The second focused upon the role of the gentry, and has become known as the "Gentry Controversy." R. H. Tawney perceived a shift of land away from crown, church and aristocracy to strengthen a new class of gentry, who sought to obtain political power commensurate with their economic status. Hugh Trevor-Roper's counter-attack suggested that, far from rising, those gentry not obtaining revenues from the Crown or the law were declining, and resented a wasteful court and royal patronage from which they were excluded. Finally, while old local histories were often scholarly narratives of the course of the war in a particular county, few of them applied serious analysis to the breakdown of consensus in the period 1640-1642: newer works, like John Morrill's *The Revolt of the Provinces* and Ronald Hutton's work on the war in the West Midlands, have thrown much-needed light upon this level of the conflict.

This flood of writing undoubtedly has an impact upon our interpretation of the formation of two opposing camps in Cornwall. The first crucial point to emerge is that in Cornwall, as elsewhere, the number of committed supporters of either party was relatively small: the majority of Cornishmen were reluctant to draw the sword. Next, lines of cleavage cannot be drawn by social class, for the war split the gentry across the nation. Religion was more influential: we should be surprised neither to find the Arundells out for the King from first to last, nor to discover that Lord Robartes felt the pull of his Puritanism stronger than gratitude for his recent peerage. Many notables had an ambivalent relationship with the Crown. Sir John Mohun had sat as MP for Grampound and warmly supported the Court party, being rewarded by appointment as Vice-Warden of the Stannaries. He was the Crown's candidate as one of the County members in 1627-8, and his defeat in the election was an index of waning Court influence. Elevated to the peerage as Lord Mohun of Okehampton, he showed his turbulent disposition first by "undue inquiries into His Majesty's debts"—for which he was fined £500—and then by brawling with another peer at the christening of James, Duke of York in 1633.

It is, at first sight, surprising that the King had a party at all. In the elections for the Long Parliament in 1640 the Duchy of Cornwall failed to secure the election of any one of the eight nominees it recommended to the Cornish boroughs under its jurisdiction, another sign of the decline of the Crown's influence at the local level.[12] The county had been heavily rated for ship-money, a tax levied ostensibly for the purpose of maintaining the navy and a source of intense irritation to the crown's opponents. Of Cornwall's 44 members of Parliament, one group, including Sir Alexander Carew and the eminent Puritan theologian Francis Rous, sided emphatically with the Parliamentary opposition to the King. The majority followed the lead of Edward Hyde, member for Saltash, in resisting the King, but most eventually drew back from the extremism of 1641-2. Yet it was not until 1641 that Cornish members began to side against the opposition: eight, amongst them Richard Arundell, Sydney Godolphin, Sir Nicholas Slanning and John Trevanion, voted against the attainder on the Earl of Strafford. Over the months that followed the split within Parliament was reflected by growing divisions in the county. One petition to Parliament made religious and constitutional demands echoing those of the parliamentary opposition: another supported the established church and hoped that the King would come to an understanding with Parliament.

Any prospect of such an understanding disappeared in early 1642. On 4 January Charles made an abortive attempt to arrest the five leaders of the opposition in the Commons, and on the 10th he left London. Parliament's Militia Ordinance, passed on the 15th, appointed deputy lieutenants, in an effort to ensure control of the militia. Unsuccessful negotiations followed until in May the King, at York began to issue Commissions of Array, appointing the most influential gentry in each county to raise the militias. On 12 August Parliament voted to raise an army and place it under the command of the Earl of Essex, and on the 22nd the royal standard was raised at Nottingham. By this stage the leading men of both parties were marshalling troops.

Mary Coate suggests that "natural conservatism, family tradition, long association with the Crown and religious sentiment" combined to draw many of the leading families in Cornwall into the Royalist ranks, and certainly most of the Arundells, Bassetts, Godolphins, Grenviles, Killigrews, Trelawnys, Trevelyans and Vyvyans stood for the King. But Parliament also had prominent supporters, amongst them Lord Robartes, Sir Richard Buller, John St Aubyn, Edmund Prideaux and John Trefusis. It was sadly typical of a nation "by the sword divided" that there were two Arundells and a Godolphin amongst the Parliamentarians. The choice of sides was rarely easy. Sir Bevil Grenvile, an experienced MP, was a well-respected and devout man who had been a close personal friend of his fellow-Cornishman, the Parliamentary leader Sir John Eliot, who had died in the Tower. But he believed that Parliament had gone too far in 1641-2, and he went home to Stowe and brought out his tenantry, in the blue and white Grenvile livery, for the King: the Royalist cause was to have few finer champions.

2: OPENING ROUNDS, 1642-43

i. Raising the Armies

An early indication of the sympathies of influential Cornishmen came when the Assizes opened at Launceston on 5 August. The chaplain who preached the assize sermon supported the King's right to raise the militia, the sheriff, John Grylls, declared that he would obey the King's commands, and went on to read the Commission of Array and the King's Proclamation against the Militia Ordinance before a large crowd, with the enthusiastic support of Warwick, Lord Mohun, who had succeeded to his father's title the previous year, Slanning, John Arundell of Trerice, Sir Bevil Grenvile and others. The Parliamentarian leaders, including Sir Richard Buller and Sir Alexander Carew, failed to persuade the judge to declare the Commissions of Array illegal, and informed Parliament of the sheriff's action. Parliament responded by summoning the Royalist leaders to appear before it: they declined, pleading the King's express command to remain in the country, and Mohun declared that it ill became his dignity as a peer to be summoned like "a common rogue."

The country's reluctance to take up arms was demonstrated by the poor turn-out at the Royalist muster on Bodmin race-course on 17 August: only 189 men appeared, most of them in the Grenvile colours. Both sides agreed to a truce on the 18th, but on the 25th a detachment of Somerset Royalists arrived at Grenvile's house at Stowe, bringing armed conflict a stage nearer. Somerset and Dorset had both declared for Parliament, and the Marquis of Hertford, the Royalist commander, had relinquished Sherborne Castle and fallen back on Minehead. Most of his force took ship for Wales, but 110 horse and 50 dragoons, with Sir Ralph Hopton, Sir Henry Killigrew and Sidney Godolphin, made for Stowe. Hopton was 44 years old in 1642, somtime a gentleman-commoner of Lincoln College Oxford, and an experienced soldier. He had served in the Elector Palatine's army and formed part of the small detachment which escorted Charles's sister Elizabeth of Bohemia—the "Winter Queen"—to safety after the defeat of her husband's forces at the Battle of the White Mountain outside Prague in 1620. In 1624 he had been lieutenant-colonel of Sir Charles Rich's Regiment, raised in England for Count Mansfeld's expedition to the Palatinate, but he declined to serve in the Cadiz expedition on the grounds that it was not properly equipped. A Puritan by religious persuasion, he had initially supported the Parliamentary opposition, but could not stomach the Militia Ordinance, and declared for the King. He was appointed lieutenant-general of the horse to the Marquis of Hertford and raised a troop of cavalry in his native Somerset at his own expense. Hertford's little army had repulsed the Earl of Bedford's much larger force from Sherborne Castle, but news of waning Royalist forces elsewhere persuaded the Marquis to leave Sherborne and make first for North Somerset, and then for Wales. Only on Hopton's advice did he send the small detachment down into Cornwall.

The Cornish Parliamentarians sought to capitalise on their comrades' success in Somerset and Dorset, and Sir Richard Buller summoned the trained bands to meet at Bodmin on 28 September to resist the Royalists who, he claimed, had invaded the country. Hopton moved faster, and reached Bodmin on the 27th, pressing on to Truro in time for the Michaelmas Assizes. The election for mayor was under way, and although the outgoing mayor refused to call out the militia for the King, his successor, prompted by Sir Richard Vyvyan, agreed. Hopton was tried for bringing an armed force into the country, honourably aquitted by the jury and thanked for his intervention. Ambrose Manaton of Launceston made a desperate attempt to secure a truce, but to no avail. On 4 October Hopton reviewed the *Posse Comitatus*—the armed force of the county—on Moilesbarrow Down. It consisted of some 4,000 untrained men, armed with the militia's often obsolete weapons, but Hopton at once organised them into regiments and set off for Launceston, where Sir Richard Buller had a much smaller Parliamentary force. Buller had hoped that the Devonshire Parliamentarians would move quickly to his support, but the townspeople of Launceston, alarmed by wild rumours moving ahead of Hopton, persuaded him to leave. The Royalists entered the town, fell to plundering, and burned Ambrose Manaton's house: it took Hopton some time to enforce order. Buller's flight left Hopton in control of Cornwall. Slanning held Pendennis for the King, Lieutenant Hannibal Bonython, governor of St Mawes, declared for Charles, and Saltash, across the Tamar from the Parliamentarian stronghold of Plymouth, was also secured by the Royalists.

The Militia's behaviour in Launceston, coupled with its marked reluctance to cross the Tamar to serve "abroad", encouraged Hopton to raise five "voluntary" regiments of foot under Grenvile, Slanning, Trevanion, William Godolphin and Lord Mohun; and Captain Edward Cosoworth raised a troop of dragoons. These were to prove some of the finest infantry raised on either side during the whole of the Civil War. They embodied all the tough independence of the Cornish character. Captain Richard Atkyns, a Gloucestershire gentleman who commanded a troop of horse in Prince Maurice's Regiment, wrote of how: "the Cornish foot could not well brook our horse (especially, when we were drawn up on corn) but they would many times let fly at us: these were the very best foot I ever saw, for marching and fighting; but so mutinous withal, that nothing but an alarm could keep them from falling foul upon their officers."[1] There may be more than a little inter-arm rivalry here, for Hopton was to lament "the extravagant disorder of the horse."[2]

The arms and equipment for the Cornish army were provided by the militia arsenals and from purchases made in France and Holland, imported through Falmouth. Slanning organised a fleet of Royalist privateers which preyed on merchantmen, giving official approval to the activities long carried out in those parts. Despite the attentions of the navy, which had adhered to Parliament, he was able to maintain an intermittent trade with the continent. Much money was raised by the sale of tin, and more was borrowed on the continent—the loan was financed by Queen Henrietta Maria's pawning the Crown Jewels in Holland. Some of Hopton's officers maintained their men at their own expense—the names Grenvile, Trelawny, Vyvyan, Trevanion and Rashleigh figure prominently amongst the contributors.

Parliament was not slow in responding to the challenge. It authorised the deputy lieutenant of Cornwall (in temporary exile across the Tamar) to raise troops, ordered the Devon Committee to support him, and sent the Earl of Bedford westwards with reinforcements. Hopton crossed the Tamar, found Exeter too well defended to be taken, and marched on Plymouth, occupying Mount Edgcumbe House and Millbrook on the Cornish side of the sound. In early December he attempted to blockade the land approaches to Plymouth, but Parliament sent supplies in by sea, and ordered Lord Robaters to raise volunteers for the city's defence. Hoping to repeat his success in Cornwall, Hopton and the High Sheriff of Devonshire summoned the Devon *Posse Comitatus* to meet at Modbury. The result was unimpressive. Hopton thought the gathering was "rather like a great fair than a posse."[3] He could barely muster enough reliable men to guard the town and send out a cavalry patrol, but the Royalists at Plympton ordered half Grenvile's regiment to join Hopton at Modbury the following morning, and patrolled the roads from Plymouth in an effort to prevent the garrison from raiding Modbury.

These precautions proved inadequate. Colonel Ruthin, a Scots professional soldier, led 800 horse and dragoons from Plymouth to Modbury under cover of darkness, dispersed the posse and captured the high sheriff and many other officers. Hopton and Slanning narrowly escaped. Ruthin gave another demonstration of his skill by falling back not on Plymouth, where he risked an ambush en route, but upon Dartmouth, which he reached safely.

Lacking the resources to take Plymouth, Hopton decided to try his luck at Exeter. The mayor, Christopher Clark, refused his summons to surrender, and although the Royalists took Alphington, Powderham and Topsham, they were unable to blockade the city effectively, and Ruthin slipped in "with a good party of Horse and musketeers mounted." A half-hearted attack on New Year's Day failed, and Hopton decided to retreat, complaining that:

Their expectation of ammunition, subsistence and increase from the County utterly failed, so as the army was enforced in that bitter season of the year (encumbered with all sorts of wants, and with disorder and general mutiny of the Foot) to retreat towards Cornwall.[4]

Hopton fell back through Crediton, Bow and Okehampton. In Bridestowe, Ruthin caught up with him, only to discover that the Cornish foot immediately "put themselves into a very excellent order of obedience beyond expectation" to repulse the attack.[5]

As the Royalists withdrew into Cornwall, the Parliamentarians grew stronger by the day. On 6 January the Earl of Stamford arrived in Exeter ahead of his main body of at least three regiments of foot. Henry Grey, 1st Earl of Stamford, was a zealous Parliamentarian who had already shown himself to be haughty, irritable and markedly hostile to the Anglican church. He was commissioned to command all forces in Hereford, Gloucestershire, Shropshire and Worcester in the absence of the Earl of Essex, and while at Gloucester he was ordered to move West to assist the local Parliamentarians. Professor J. Simmons has noted that Stamford's appointment was based solely on his rank and wealth, and took no account of his cantankerous nature, his ignorance of the West Country and his military inexperience.[6] Ruthin, now a general, had bombarded the Royalist outpost of Saltash by both land and sea. An attempt at landing under the cover of this bombardment was repulsed by Trevanion and Captain William Arundell, but news of Parliamentarian reinforcements persuaded the Royalists to fall back first on Liskeard and then on Lostwithiel. Colonel William Strode secured the crossings of the Tamar at New Bridge, Gunnislake, and marched on to join Ruthin, who concentrated at Liskeard.

Ruthin's subsequent action was to bring him into disrepute. Conventional wisdom suggests that he should have waited until Stamford arrived, when the united force should have been more than a match for the Royalists. He decided not to do so, either because he was anxious not to be superseded by Stamford, or, not unreasonably, because he did not wish to give his opponents time to recover. But recover they did. On 17 January a storm drove three Parliamentarian vessels, crammed with arms and money, into Falmouth, and when Hopton's army mustered on Moilesbarrow Down it was well-armed and had a fortnight's advance of pay in its pockets. The Royalists advanced at once, without heavy guns or baggage, and bivouacked in Lord Mohun's Park at Boconnoc. That night they held a council of war and resolved to attack Ruthin, whether they found him in the field or in Liskeard. The Western army was jointly commanded, under the King's commission, by Mohun, Hopton, Sir John Berkeley, (a Member of Parliament with much military and diplomatic experience), and Colonel William Ashburnham, or by any two of them. The council set this arrangement aside, offering to serve under Hopton's sole command.

ii. The Battle of Braddock Down, 19 January 1643

The ground over which the Battle of Braddock Down was fought has altered a good deal since 1643, largely because of the "emparkment" of Boconnoc in the 18th Century. Moreover, local tradition which associates earthworks in the area with batteries erected for the battle or burial-pits dug after it is almost certainly wrong. In 1643 the ground was far more open than it is now, though the roads were hedged, and there were enclosures elsewhere. Ruthin had deployed on "a pretty rising ground in the way towards Liskeard," almost certainly just south-west of Braddock Church, with musketeers lining the hedges on the road from Braddock to the main Liskeard road. Hopton drew up his army on the high ground north-east of Boconnoc, in an area pitted by ancient earthworks and marked by a stone monument which pre-dates the battle. He pushed an advanced guard, known, in 17th Century military parlance, as a forlorn hope, into some hedged enclosures in front of his main position. His horse and dragoons were posted on the flanks, and his only artillery—two small iron drakes, brought up covertly from Lord Mohun's house, were posted on his left flank, just out of musket-shot of Ruthin's line and screened from it by horse.

Neither side had a clear advantage in numbers: Ruthin had more horse than his opponents, but Hopton had more foot, and the Parliamentarian artillery was slow in arriving. For about two hours the advanced elements of each army exchanged shots, but neither commander was anxious to leave his high ground. It was not in Hopton's interest to play a waiting game, for the Parliamentarians had ample supplies of food and could afford to hold their ground, while the morale of his own Cornish might ebb if the waiting went on too long. Accordingly, he decided to attack. Prayers were said at the head of each unit—"mass" according to the Parliamentarians—and the whole army charged. The two drakes on Hopton's left fired a salvo: they were probably within case-shot range, and the psychological shock helped unnerve Ruthin's troops. The attack of Grenvile's Regiment was especially awe-inspiring. Sir Bevil led it down the slope and up the rising ground on the far side, his men bellowing "A Grenvile! A Grenvile!", his griffin colour borne by the seven-foot Anthony Payne.

The sight was too much for Ruthin's men, who got off one volley and took to their heels. Panic seized the Parliamentarians. "Both our horse and foot," wrote one, "were suddenly routed, and every man divided and dispersed, ran and rode as fast as fear could carry them towards Saltash."[7] There was an ugly scramble in the Liskeard road as the townsmen joined the horse on the Royalist left wing in harrying the fugitives. Some 200 Parliamentarians were slain and 1,250 captured. The Royalists took all Ruthin's ammunition and baggage, and five guns. One was a saker, but the remainder were all brass and included a 14-foot long piece with the Tudor Rose and Crown engraved on it, probably an unusually long culverin. The two 12-pounders captured at Braddock Down were the mainstay of Hopton's artillery for many a long year. The Royalists admitted the loss of only two men, and Grenvile's Regiment as its commander wrote happily to his wife, "lost not a man."[8]

iii. The Equipoise of Fortune: January—May 1643

Hopton briefly rested his army at Liskeard, and on 21 January divided his forces. Berkeley, Granvile and Slanning were dispatched with half the horse and dragoons to face Stamford, who had withdrawn from Launceston to Tavistock on hearing of the disaster at Braddock, while Hopton and Mohun marched on Saltash, where Ruthin had taken refuge. On the late afternoon Sunday 22 January Hopton assaulted Saltash, the Parliamentarians resisting strongly from an earthwork, mounting four guns, before the main gate, and receiving fire support from a 16-gun warship lying inshore. By nightfall Ruthin's powder was running low, and he tried to withdraw. Getting his men into boats on a winter evening, with the Royalists pressing into the town behind them, was no easy task: many of the boats were overloaded, and Ruthin lost as many men by drowning as he had in battle. As it was, the Royalists captured 120 men and 20 guns, and Plymouth hourly expected attack.

Yet the Parliamentarian position was not as desperate as it seemed. Although the Royalists blockaded the town, Stamford had marched in from Tavistock before the ring closed, the mayor was an energetic and loyal Parliamentarian, and the city could still be supplied by sea. If the Parliamentarians could not mount an offensive from Plymouth, neither could the Royalists take the city, for the Cornish militia had declined to cross the Tamar, leaving Hopton short of troops. On 29 January commissioners from each side met at Robert Trelawney's house at Ham, near Plymouth, to discuss a truce, but negotiations collapsed over Hopton's demand that the city's new fortifications should be dismantled and the old ones surrendered to the King. On the following day the Cornish mounted what Parliamentarian news-sheets depicted as a full-scale assault, but was probably an attack on an outpost, for there is no sign of the casualty-list that a major attack would have implied.

In the meantime, the Devon Committee, the deputy lieutenants and prominent local Parliamentarians were raising troops in North Devon to come to the aid of Plymouth. On the night of 7-8 February Berkeley, Ashburnham and Grenvile, with a party of mounted men, rode out from the Royalist lines at Plympton in an attempt to disperse them. They reached Tavistock and found it empty, and rode on to Okehampton. There they decided to press on to Totnes, and Berkeley and Ashburnham set off with the horse while Grenvile followed with the dragoons. Just after dawn, in the village of

Chagford, Berkeley collided with an enemy force under Sir John Northcote which had arrived some hours before. The Parliamentarians stood to their arms stoutly, and Berkeley's men had to cut their way out. Their greatest loss was the poet and philosopher Sidney Godolphin, hit just above the knee as he rode through the village: he cried "O God, I am hurt," and fell dead. Born in 1610, he was the second son of Sir William Godolphin, and had sat for Helston in the Long Parliament. Slight in build and melancholy by nature, he had warned Parliament of the chancy nature of war, but when it came he served enthusiastically as one of the King's Commissioners of Array, and, for all his courtly elegance, took to living in the field with "courage and alacrity." Despite his inexperience, his advice was greatly valued, and the Royalist leaders were downcast by his loss. Grenvile wrote sadly that "he was as gallant a gent as the world had," and Hopton thought him "as perfect an absolute piece of virtue as ever our nation bred."[9] The Royalists brought his body away, and he lies buried in the chancel of Okehampton church.

    The seige of Plymouth went badly. As Grenvile himself recognised, the Royalists had little hope of taking the city as long as it could be supplied by sea, and in the rear of their lines growing numbers of Devonshire peasantry joined the Parliamentarians. On 20 February a Parliamentarian force of some 9,000 men had assembled at Kingsbridge, and on the 21st it attacked the Slanning and Trevanion's Regiments, 2,000 in all, in their solid position at Modbury. The battle went on all afternoon and evening. The Cornish fought stubbornly, and had to be prised back, hedge by hedge, into the town, whose buildings were soon ablaze. Slanning managed to withdraw most of his force under the cover of darkness, but lost 100 killed, 150 prisoners, 1,100 muskets and five guns. This reverse coincided with an attack by Stamford's forces from within the city upon two Royalist regiments at Stoke, and Hopton decided to raise the siege.

    The withdrawal was well executed: Hopton got most of his guns to Saltash, and the horse and foot concentrated on Tavistock. It suited both parties to agree to a temporary truce in March and April, and its conclusion found the Royalists behind the Tamar, raising money from the gentlemen and freeholders of Cornwall, with a general muster of the army ordered for Launceston on Sunday 23 April, the day after the truce expired. Stamford raised more troops and took 2,000 seamen into his army, but the end of the truce found him immobilised by gout in Exeter. James Chudleigh, third son of Lieutenant-General Sir George Chudleigh, a Devonshire baronet and leading member of the County Committee for Devon, was only twenty-five years old but had seen service in Ireland. He was major general of foot to the Earl of Stamford, and command devolved upon him when the Earl fell sick.

Chudleigh left Lifton on 22 April with 1,500 musketeers, 200 pikemen, five troops of horse and some guns. His scouts told him that there were few Royalists and no cannon in Launceston, and he decided to attack as soon as the truce expired, before the Royalist muster was complete. Hopton knew of the presence of the enemy at Lifton, and was uncomfortably aware that he had only Grenvile's Regiment of 1,200 to hold Launceston until the rest of the army marched in from its positions along the line of the Tamar. He posted a small party of dragoons to hold Polston Bridge, and as soon as his men had attended church he drew up his army on Beacon Hill, dominating the eastern approaches to the town. He lined the hedges at its foot with musketeers, but even after the arrival of Godolphin's Regiment he was outnumbered by Chudleigh: the initial Parliamentarian attacks beat the Royalist musketeers back from hedge to hedge, and Hopton had no answer to Chudleigh's guns.

The tide turned towards mid-morning, when Lord Mohun's Regiment, led by its major, Sir Walter Slingsby, marched up, and Berkeley brought in the horse and dragoons. Hopton tried to slip three troops of horse and a regiment of foot round Chudleigh's flank to sieze Polston Bridge but this move was thwarted by the arrival of Parliamentarian reinforcements: 700 grey-coats of Sir John Merrick's London Regiment under their lieutenant-colonel, and a detachment of Sir John Northcote's Devonshire men, led by their major and the Earl of Stamford's energetic chaplain.

The reinforcements enabled Chudleigh to hold Polston Bridge against the Royalist horse, but at about 7.00pm Slanning and Trevanion arrived with their regiments and Hopton mounted a determined attack with three columns of foot led by himself, Berkeley and Major General Thomas Bassett. Chudleigh's men were exhausted and outnumbered, and he decided to fall back. It is to the credit of this youthful and inspiring commander that he brought his tired men off in good order, himself harnessing oxen to a gun when one of his officers declared that it would have to be abandoned. Hopton was in no position to pursue: his troops became mutinous, and the accidental explosion of some gunpowder further dampened their spirits. Amongst their casualties were Captain James Bassett, brother of Francis Bassett of Tehidy, and one the Arundell clan, Ensign James Arundell.[10]

On 25 April Hopton heard from a sympathiser in Okehampton that Chudleigh's force was in great disorder, and set off in the early evening with the intention of surprising Okehampton the following morning. The little army marched out in good order, with 300 horse and 300 dragoons in the van and rear, 3,000 foot and four guns, including two of the Braddock Down 12-pounders. Chudleigh's scoutmaster, who should have obtained warning of the Royalist approach, failed to do so, but a quartermaster in search for billets saw some of Hopton's scouts and raised the alarm. Chudleigh, who now had only 109 horse and 1,000 foot, held a quick council of war, and decided to ambush the Royalists with his horse to give the foot time to escape.

Chudleigh took his horse onto Sourton Down, between Okehampton and Bridestowe, divided them into six groups, and deployed them along a fold in the ground. As Hopton's army approached, full of confidence, with Hopton and Mohun chatting lightheartedly at the head of the leading dragoons, they were fired upon, and Captain Drake charged them with his 36 men, shouting "Fall on, Fall on, they run, they run!" The Royalist advanced guard broke and galloped into their foot, throwing it into confusion. Mohun and Grenvile made a stand by the guns, and Hopton sent word to Slanning to bring up the rearguard. Eventually Hopton and his officers rallied part of the foot on an ancient earthworks, with the cannon on its slopes and musketeers in the ditch around it. Chudleigh had sent back to Okehampton for his foot to join him to exploit this success, but they were deterred by the fire from the earthwork, and many of them slipped away in the darkness. The most that Chudleigh could do was to leave matches burning on the gorse-bushes to persuade the Royalists that he still held his ground, while he tried to reassemble his men back in Okehampton. The Cornish began a painful retreat on Bridestowe, but a fierce thunder-storm threw them into confusion: it was a bad end to an operation marred by over-confidence. Chudleigh had captured 20 men, 1,000 muskets and 100 horses, together with Hopton's personal papers containing much useful information. Mohun had narrowly escaped capture, and Henry Carey, the newly-appointed High Sheriff of Devonshire, crept home disguised as a woman.

A letter from the King captured in Hopton's baggage revealed that the Cornish Royalists had orders to march into Somerset, to join the Royalist army there under Lord Hertford. The junction between the two Royalist forces would have altered the balance of power in the south-west, and Stamford, his health vastly improved by the news of Sourton Down, decided to prevent it. He sent Sir George Chudleigh with 1,200 of his 1,400 horse to Bodmin, to surprise the sheriff who was assembling the *Posse Comitatus* there, and drew together all the forces that could be spared from garrison duty in Devon in a general rendezvous at Torrington. He had 5,400 foot, 200 horse and 13 guns when he crossed the border on the Holsworthy-Stratton road on 15 May.

Hopton's regiments were widely spread—Mohun at Liskeard, Slanning at Saltash, Trevanion at Launceston and Grenvile at Stratton. New troops were raised, and the sheriff, Francis Bassett, made frantic efforts to find money to pay them. But by the time garrisons had been left to hold key posts, Hopton had only 2,400 foot and 500 horse. He felt that his own shortage of supplies and the imminent risk of invasion meant that he had no alternative but to find Stamford and attack him, and on 13 May his army bivouacked in the open on the common at North Petherwin, in remarkably good heart.

iv. The Battle of Stratton, 16 May 1643

Stamford's failings as a soldier were considerable, but even to his untutored eye the high ground—now called Stamford Hill—just west of the main Bideford road on the northern outskirts of Stratton was an impressive position. The hill, rising to more than 200 feet above sea level, is the finger-tip of a ridge stretching down from the North. The tiny River Neet flowed at the foot of its precipitous Eastern slopes, and Grunshill Wood formed a robust barrier between the river and the crest. To the West, towards Bude, the slope was gentler, but the road which ran from Stratton across the hill wound up a steep slope to the south of the wood. A semi-circular earthwork, probably of prehistoric origin, stood between the wood and the Stratton road. Stamford took up position on the hill, putting his guns in the earthwork and lining the hedges with his musketeers.

The Royalists advanced from North Petherwin by way of Week St Mary, and crossed the Neet at Efford Mill, just south of Stratton. The army spent the night of 15-16 May in enclosures between the river and the lower slopes of the hill. Hopton took up his quarters in the Old Manor House—now the Tree Inn—in Stratton itself, where a council of war "quickly resolved, notwithstanding the great visible disadvantage, that they must either force the Enemies' Camp, while the most part of their horse and dragoons were from them, or unavoidably perish."[11]

Musketry squibbed out amongst the hedges at dawn, and at 5.00 am Hopton gave the order to attack. The foot formed four columns, each about 600 strong with two cannon. Hopton and Mohun were to attack from the south, up the Stratton road; Berkeley and Grenvile attacked from the south-west, Bassett and Godolphin from the west, and Slanning and Trevanion from the north. Colonel John Digby, with 300 horse and dragoons, covered the left rear of Hopton's army, on a sandy common that is now

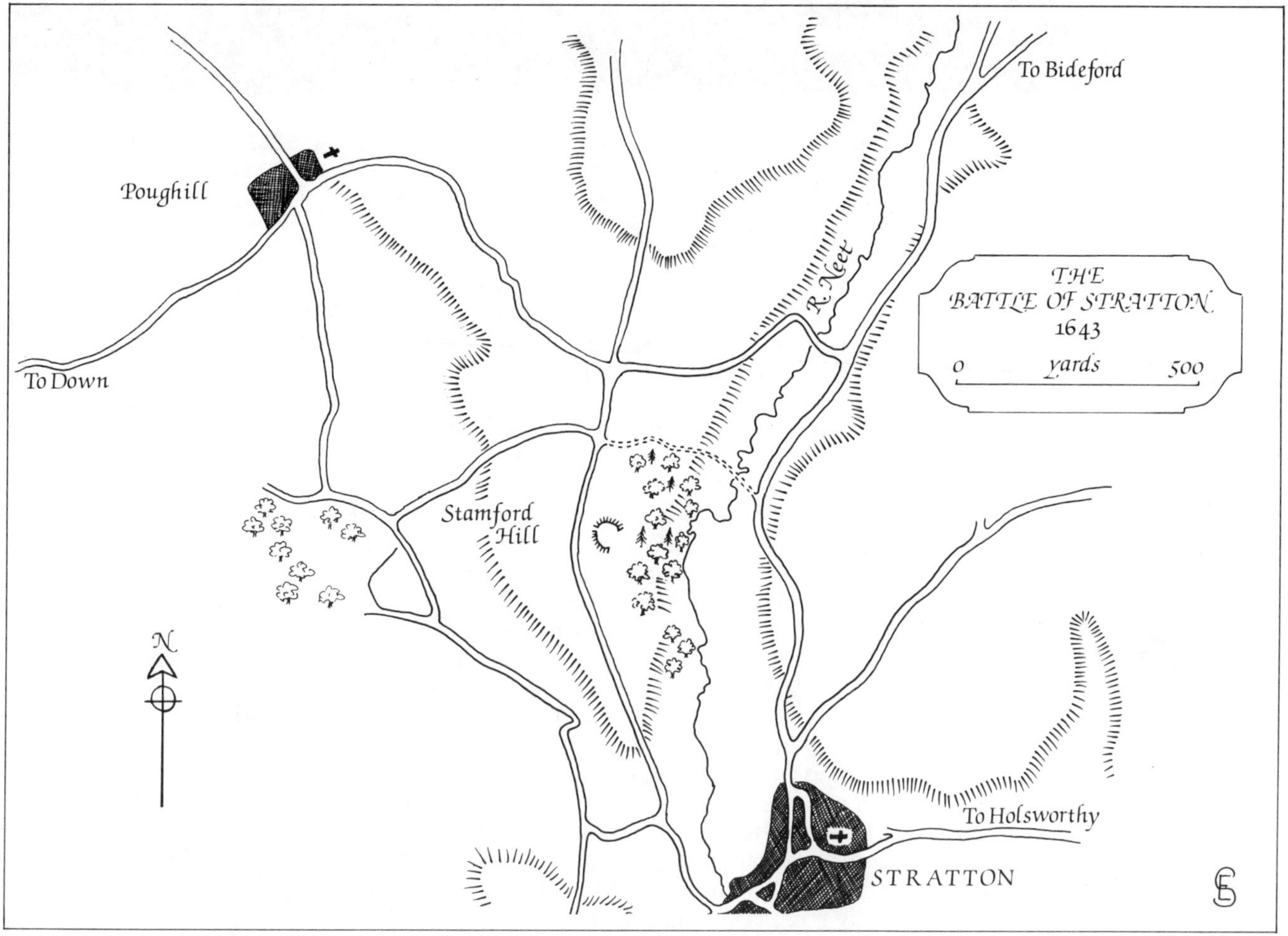
THE
BATTLE OF STRATTON
1643
0 yards 500
To Bideford
Poughill
R. Neet
To Down
Stamford
Hill
N
To Holsworthy
STRATTON

Bude golf course. The fighting went on all day, with repeated attacks up the hill being repulsed with loss, until, at about 3.00pm, Hopton was told that he had only four barrels of powder left. He and his senior officers then resolved to advance without firing until they reached the crest, and the moral effect of their advance with the cold steel persuaded some of the Parliamentarians to flee. Major-General Chudleigh put himself at the head of a body of pikemen and briskly counter-attacked a stand of pikes led by Grenvile, throwing it into disorder: Grenvile was knocked down in the mêlée. Berkeley quickly supported him with the musketeers of their column, killing most of their assailants and capturing Chudleigh.

The Parliamentarians began to give way quickly. Robert Bennett of Hexworthy, an officer of Sir Samuel Rolle's Devonshire regiment, complained that "the enemy came in upon our rear by reason that the left wing failed", so it was probably the attack of the two southernmost columns that proved decisive, rolling up the Parliamentarian line along the plateau. The four columns met on the open ground at the top of the hill, turning some of the captured cannon upon their former owners, and pushing on to take Stamford's baggage train. The victorious Cornish celebrated their victory with "public prayers upon the place", and spend the night amongst the spoils, which included 70 barrels of powder and plentiful food. Stamford had lost 300 killed and 1,700 prisoners, 13 cannon, a mortar and all his baggage, which contained £5,000.

Stamford beat a retreat to Bideford, and thence to Exeter, where he was soon to be besieged. Clarendon suggests that he had left the field in haste, having taken care not to expose his person, but Colonel John Weare, an eyewitness who commanded a Devonshire regiment, saw him with a small group of followers trying to stem the Cornish rush. In any event the earl soon found a scapegoat. Chudleigh was taken off to Oxford, but had been so impressed by what he saw of the Cornish—or disgusted by Stamford's lacklustre performance—that he joined the Royalist army, only to be mortally wounded as a colonel of foot at the capture of Dartmouth on 6 October 1643. Stamford speedily complained that Chudleigh had betrayed him, and had actually charged him during the battle, but from other accounts it is clear that this was a calumny against a brave and enterprising officer. Sir George Chudleigh hastily withdrew from Bodmin as soon as he heard of the disaster, but lost many men to enraged townspeople and peasantry on his withdrawal. He resigned his commission when he heard of his son's defection, and transferred his allegiance to the King shortly afterwards.[12]

3: TRIUMPH AND TRAGEDY: THE CORNISH ABROAD, 1643

Leaving Cornwall secure behind him, Hopton marched on to Launceston, where he received orders to join Prince Maurice and the Marquis of Hertford, who had advanced into Somerset. Exeter refused his summons to surrender, so he continued to Chard, where he met Maurice and Hertford on 4 June. His army consisted of 3,000 foot and 500 horse, 300 dragoons and 5 guns, its morale boosted by victory at Stratton and its confidence never higher. But the union with Hertford's force was not entirely happy. Hopton observed that the ill behaviour of the Royalist horse alienated opinion in Somerset, and he found himself junior to Hertford and Maurice. The former was fifty-four years old, and loved his ease and his books, but had been made lieutenant-general of the six Western counties because of his social position and reputation for loyalty. Maurice was the King's nephew, and although he had attracted less attention than his more flamboyant brother Rupert, he was not without experience, having served with the Swedes in the Upper Palatinate and beaten Sir William Waller at Ripple Field in April 1643.

The combined army occupied Taunton, Bridgewater and Dunster Castle, and marched on Wells to intercept the Somerset Parliamentarians, who were on their way to join Waller's army at Bath. Waller was one of the most capable generals on Parliament's side. He had been in the Venetian service as a young man, and had fought the Imperialists in Bohemia and the Palatinate. Forty-five years old in 1643, he had sat for Andover in the Long Parliament, was a personal friend of Hopton's, and shared his religious views.

On 10 June the Royalists got the worst of a cavalry skirmish at Chewton Mendip. They spent a fortnight at Wells, and on 2 July they marched to Bradford-on-Avon, moving thence to Monkton Farleigh in an effort to outflank Bath from the East. After inconclusive fighting, on 4 July they set off for Lansdown Hill which dominates Bath from the North, only to discover Waller securely ensconced on top of it. Attacking Lansdown offered poor prospects, and the council of war decided to retreat on Marshfield. This induced Waller to swing his army onto the northern end of

Lansdown, where he threw up emplacements for his guns, while his cavalry drove in the Royalist pickets in front of Marshfield. The Royalists rose to this affront by advancing on Lansdown, and, after heavy skirmishing along the road from Marshfield to Bath, the battle became general.

Initial attacks on Waller's formidable position made little headway, and things looked decidedly black for the Royalists when Grenvile advanced at the head of his own regiment. A determined attack took him onto the rim of the hill, where he was charged three times by the Parliamentarian horse. In the last charge Grenvile was struck down by a poll-axe, and fell, mortally wounded. His eldest son, fifteen-year-old John, had a commission in his regiment, and the gigantic Anthony Payne is said to have swung John up into his father's empty saddle and given him his sword. The Cornish, in grief and rage, surged over the Parliamentarian defences, and Waller's men fell back a short distance. Losses in the Royalist army had been appalling. But Waller, too, had suffered severely, and in the early hours of the morning he slipped away to Bath, leaving the Royalists free to retreat to Marshfield and on to Chippenham, with Hopton, badly injured by an accidental explosion, travelling in a bed in Hertford's coach.

After a two-day halt in Chippenham the Royalists left for Devizes on 9 July, with Waller close behind: on the 10th Waller drew up his whole army on Roundway Down, north of the town, but the Royalists, desperately short of ammunition, declined to give battle. That night a council of war resolved that Hertford and Maurice would break out with the cavalry and ride for Oxford to fetch help, leaving Hopton to defend Devizes. The cavalry duly got clear, and on the 11th Waller surrounded the town.

Maurice and Hertford reached Oxford on the 11th, and heard that the King had already sent the Earl of Crawford off with a convoy of ammunition—in fact this was mauled by Waller's cavalry between Marlborough and Devizes—and Lord Wilmot had also left with his brigade of horse. Hertford remained in Oxford to recover from his exertions. Maurice's men, reinforced by Sir John Byron's brigade, retraced their steps, and met Wilmot, and the survivors of Crawford's detachment, at Marlborough on 12 July. On the following day the relieving force totally defeated Waller on Roundway Down, although the Cornish foot, marching up from Devizes, arrived too late to play any significant part in the battle.

Waller's defeat altered the complexion of the war in the south-west. It persuaded the King to send reinforcements from his main army at Oxford, and on 15 July Prince Rupert left the city with three brigades of foot under Lord Grandison, Colonel Henry Wentworth and Colonel John Belasyse, two cavalry brigades under Major-General Sir Arthur Aston and Colonel Charles Gerard, and nine troops of dragoons under Colonel Henry Washington. Hopton and Maurice, meanwhile, had entered Bath, whose garrison had departed for Bristol. Waller had taken the remnants of his army up to Gloucester, slipping off to Evesham, and thence to London, on Rupert's approach.

Rupert's first objective was Bristol, held for Parliament by Colonel Nathaniel Fiennes, son of the Parliamentarian peer Lord Saye and Sele. Fiennes had 300 horse and 1,500 foot, was well supported by the townsmen, and nearly 100 guns were mounted in the city's defences. These comprised an inner ring following the line of the Rivers Avon and Frome, and an outer ring of rampart and ditch connecting Water Fort, Brandon Hill Fort, Windmill Hill Fort, Colston's Mount and Prior's Hill Fort. From there the defences ran south-east to the Frome and on to Lawford's Gate, then south-west to the Avon. The south-eastern segment ran from Tower Harratz on the river, to Temple Gate and back up to the river near Redcliffe Gate.

Rupert conducted a reconnaissance of 23 July, leaving Washington to hold Clifton Hill to the West of the city. Maurice's men established themselves opposite the south-eastern sector and began to throw up batteries. On 24 July Fiennes refused a summons to surrender, and, after much debate, the Royalists decided to storm the city at dawn on the 26th. The signal for the assault was to be the firing of two demi-cannon from Lord Grandison's battery, and on hearing it Rupert's three brigades would go forward, Grandison against Stokes Croft and Prior's Hill Fort, Belasyse against Windmill Hill, and Wentworth into a re-entrant between Brandon Hill and Windmill Hill Forts. Maurice's foot formed three columns. Slanning led 500 Cornish foot in the centre, attacking Temple Gate; Sir Thomas Bassett had Grenvile's and Godolphin's Regiments on his left, and Colonel Brutus Buck took Hertford's infantry forward on Slanning's right.

Things went wrong from the start. The Cornish attacked at 3.00am, without waiting for the signal, and the slaughter was terrible as they rushed for the ditch and rampart. Their scaling-ladders were too short to reach up out of the ditch, and although cart-loads of faggots, and empty wagons, had been collected to help fill it in, they failed to do so. The officers, leading with reckless courage, fell in scores. Colonel Buck mounted the rampart but was struck off by a halberd and died in the ditch. Slanning and Trevanion fell mortally wounded within yards of one another, Bassett was wounded, and Slingsby, pushing a cart into the ditch, fell in after it and was carried off unconscious.

Fortune had been kinder to the Royalists north of the river. Although Grandison and Belasyse had made no headway, Wentworth's men had forced an entry between Brandon Hill and Windmill Hill, and were soon supported by part of Belasyse's brigade and horse under Aston. The fight for Frome Gate, in the inner ring of defences, lasted two hours. Belasyse was badly wounded and Colonel Henry Lunsford killed, but the arrival of some of Grandison's men clinched the business, and the Royalists fought their way in. Fiennes asked for terms, and articles of surrender were agreed that night.

Bristol was a valuable prize, but it had been dearly won. The Oxford army lamented young Lord Grandison, Henry Lunsford and Nathaniel Moyle. The loss of Slanning and Trevanion, coming so soon after the death of Grenvile, deeple shocked the Cornish and filled the King's enemies with delight:

Gone the four wheels of Charles's wain

Grenvile, Godolphine, Slanning, Trevanion slain . . .

Mary Coate, combining painstaking research with penetrating feel for the period

Sir Bevil Grenvile (1596-1643).

Sir William Balfour (d-1660).
Balfour is shown wearing Cuirassier armour and carrying a Pole Axe.

Ralph, Lord Hopton (1598-1652).

Henry Grey, 1st Earl of Stamford (1599-1673).

Robert Devereux, 3rd Earl of Essex (1591-1646).

Stratton: The Parliamentarian position from the West.

Stratton: *The monument in the centre of Stamford's position.*

Respryn Bridge, *looking downstream.*

King Charles I

Restormel: The shell keep held by Colonel John Weare's Regiment.

Restormel: the splayed embrasure above the chapel.

St Nectan's Chapel, between Lostwithiel and Boconnoc, lost its tower in the fighting which preceded the Royalist occupation of Beacon Hill.

Anthony Payne (c 1612-1691) Painted by Sir Godfrey Kneller in 1680 at the command of Charles II.

The Lostwithiel—Fowey road as seen from Castle Dore. Stout hedges like this provided excellent cover for the Parliamentarian musketeers, and were the scene of heavy fighting on 31 August.

St Bartholomew's Church, Lostwithiel. The line of the old roof, lifted when the Parliamentarians exploded gunpowder beneath it in 1644, can be seen on the spire.

Lostwithiel Bridge. The high ground on the horizon was occupied by Maurice's men on 21 August 1644.

Pendennis Castle: Paul Ivey's late Elizabethan defences. The guns behind these embrasures fired out towards St Mawes.

Pendennis Castle: The Keep.

Kilkhampton Church: Sir Bevil Grenvile's memorial.

47

which sometimes eludes academic historians, wrote:
> the army which Grenvile and Hopton had led so triumphantly across the Tamar after Stratton had perished as surely as if it had fallen with Grenvile on the heights of Lansdowne, or with Slanning by the walls of Bristol. For the life of the Cornish army had been in its leaders; they had inspired it with enthusiasm, they had given it its unity, and when they died its history ended.[1]

4: THE LOSTWITHIEL CAMPAIGN 1644

i. The Tilting Balance: July 1643-July 1644

The fall of Bristol offered golden opportunities to the King's council of war, and after much debate, Charles and Rupert set off for Gloucester. Its defences were not much stronger than those of Bristol, and, left to his own devices, Rupert might have attempted a storm, but memories were fresh, and the Royalists began a siege. Parliament sent the Earl of Essex to the city's relief, and on 8 September he entered it in the nick of time, for the garrison was all but out of ammunition. The Royalists positioned themselves between Essex and the captial: the resulting First Battle of Newbury, fought on 20 September, was drawn, but the Royalists fell back on Oxford, allowing Essex to return to London.

Fortunes elsewhere were mixed. Caernarvon subdued Dorset, though he could not take Lyme. Maurice, promoted to replace Hertford—tactfully recalled to Oxford to give the King the benefit of his counsel—dispersed the Devonshire Parliamentarians: Exeter surrendered on 6 September and Dartmouth on 5 October. Plymouth was blockaded in August, and in mid-October Maurice established a formal siege. He abandoned it in late December, but maintained a blockade, and in the New Year his grip tightened again.

A new Grenvile appeared on the scene. Sir Richard, Bevil's younger brother, had served on the continent, and commanded a regiment destined for the relief of La Rochelle in 1627. He married a rich widow, but after dispute with his brother-in-law, from which Grenvile emerged with little credit, the marriage was dissolved and Grenvile was imprisoned. He then served in Ireland, only returning in August 1643. Arrested by the Parliamentarian authorities and sent to London, he was eventually given arrears of pay and cash to raise a regiment of horse. On 6 March 1644 he turned up in Oxford with 36 of his troop, £600, and news of a Parliamentarian scheme for surprising Basing House. He was sent to assist Colonel John Digby before Plymouth, and when Digby was wounded he assumed command. If Bevil had inherited all that was best in the Grenvile character, Richard was its darker embodiment. He was cruel and ruthless, with a sharp tongue and distaste for subordination.

In October further to the east, Hopton, elevated to the peerage as Baron Hopton of Stratton, was ordered to clear Dorset, Wiltshire and Hampshire, "and so to point forwards as far as he could go towards London". He secured most of Hampshire, and on 9 December took Arundel Castle. This proved the high-water mark of his success. Waller destroyed a detachment in Alton on 13 December, and on 6 January recaptured Arundel. Hopton was reinforced by the King's general, Lord Forth, and Essex sent a cavalry brigade under Sir William Balfour to strengthen Waller. The armies met at Cheriton on 29 March, and the Royalists were defeated in a battle which opened direct communications between London and the West country.

Cheriton was a bad start to the King's campaigning year, and the shape of things to come elsewhere. The Marquis of Newcastle, commanding Royalist forces in the North, had made slow progress, though he had beaten Lord Fairfax and his son Sir Thomas at Adwalton Moor in June 1643, and laid siege to Hull. However, the Earl of Manchester, assisted by young Fairfax and an enterprising East Anglian cavalry officer, Oliver Cromwell, routed a detachment of Newcastle's at Winceby on 11 October, on the same day that a sortie from Hull persuaded the Marquis to break up the siege. By the late spring of 1644 he was in even greater difficulties, for the Scots army, taking the field in alliance with Parliament, had crossed the Tweed in January, and April saw it, in conjunction with the Fairfaxes, besiege Newcastle's army in York. Rupert manoeuvred his way through to the city to join Newcastle, but their combined armies were soundly defeated by the Scots and English at Marston Moor on 2 July.

Charles had retained a substantial army based on Oxford. In the spring of 1644 Parliamentarian leaders considered making a joint attack with Essex's army from London and Manchester's from East Anglia, but the project foundered, and it was not until April that Essex and Waller began to move against Oxford. Charles slipped out, eluded his pursuers and reached Worcester ahead of them. On 6 June Waller and Essex met, and the Earl decided that Waller should remain in the Midlands to deal with the

King, while he marched into the West Country to relieve Lyme and Plymouth. By the time the Committee of Both Kingdoms, which controlled the Anglo-Scottish war effort, heard about this it was too late to intervene. Waller misjudged an attack on the King at Cropredy Bridge, near Banbury, on 29 June, and was beaten. The King's council of war was uncertain how to exploit this victory. Charles had previously sent his pregnant Queen Henrietta Maria to Exeter, and on 12 July he set off to join her in the West. That very night he heard Rupert's news of the catastrophe of Marston Moor, but he pressed on westwards.

ii Essex moves West

Essex had reached Blandford when, on 14 June, he received word from the Committee of Both Kingdoms, ordering him to send a party of horse to relieve Lyme and to return to Oxfordshire with his foot. He declined to obey, arguing that cavalry alone could not raise the siege, and that if he retreated it would look as if he had been defeated. Robert Devereux, 3rd Earl of Essex, had commanded a foot regiment in the Dutch service, and Clarendon wrote that in 1640 he was "the most popular man in the kingdom, the darling of the sword-men".[1] Appointed general of Parliament's army on 12 July 1642, he had commanded it in the war's first battle at Edgehill, and the relief of Gloucester was his most creditable achievement to date. His relationship with Parliament was not altogether happy, and he strenuously objected to local armies being given resources which he was denied. Nevertheless, he was unfailingly loyal to Parliament, personally brave, and popular with his men, amongst whom his appearance often provoked cheers of "Hey for Robin!".

In the event, Essex's decision to march West was disastrous. But there was some logic behind it. The energetic Francis Bassett raised money in Cornwall by sequestering the estates of Parliamentarians and levying taxes, although Cornish enthusiasm had waned after Lansdown and Bristol. Nevertheless, the county made a useful financial contribution to the Royalist cause, and money was coined in mints at

Truro and Exeter. Privateers sallied out of Cornish harbours to attack shipping, the export of tin helped to pay for the King's munitions, and with Cornwall solid for the King there remained the risk that Plymouth would fall. Indeed, in August 1644 a plot by its governor, Sir Alexander Carew, to betray the city was narrowly thwarted. The Queen was in Exeter, where she gave birth to a daughter, and her capture might have proved influential. Finally, Lord Robartes, who accompanied Essex, assured the Earl that Cornwall could comfortably support his army.

Essex succeeded in his first objective, raising the siege of Lyme on 15 June, and moving on to take Weymouth and Bridport. He marched on through Somerset and into Devon, reaching Tavistock on 23 July. Grenvile at once broke up the siege of Plymouth, collected local garrisons, and fell back to hold the crossings of the Tamar at Horsebridge. Encouraged by Robartes, who greatly over-estimated his own influence in the county, Essex decided to push on. On 26 July he brushed Grenvile's force aside, and on the 28th he reached Bodmin.

The Royalists were not far behind. Maurice abandoned the siege of Lyme and concentrated on Exeter, drawing in 1,000 Somerset levies, 1,500 newly-raised Cornishmen and 800 foot from the garrison of Bristol to bring his army to nearly 12,000 men. The King's army, about 7,000 strong, reached Exeter on 26 July, and although Charles was too late to meet his wife, who had departed for Falmouth, and thence for France, on 30 June, he had at least the satisfaction of seeing his baby daughter.

For the Royalists the strategic situation was quite encouraging. Grenvile fell back before the Parliamentarians, and if his levies were unable to face Essex in open field, they made it difficult for the Earl's men to forage. The Cornish peasantry may not have been enthusiastic about the war, but they resented the presence of invaders from across the Tamar, and the Parliamentarians found themselves starved of intelligence and provisions. The converse was true. To the King's personal prestige was added the fact that he had many of the local gentry with him, and supplies and information flowed in. On 4 August, for instance, a small boy told a party of Royalist horse "that there were many gay men in Lord Mohun's house at Boconnoc", and in the ensuing surprise several officers were captured: Essex's quartermaster-general escaped disguised as a servant. It was only good knowledge of the ground and widespread local support—strengthened by the application of unusually strict discipline to prevent pillaging—that made the remaining Royalist manoeuvres possible. They were extraordinarily complex by the standards of the 17th Century, when communications hinged upon written messages or the spoke word, and the operations of detached forces often came to grief because of misunderstood signals or delayed orders.

On 2 August Essex marched from Bodmin to Lostwithiel, sending a force to secure the port of Fowey in an effort to ensure communications with the fleet, under the Earl of Warwick. A day later Charles ordered Grenvile to move up from Penryn to Tregony to obstruct Essex's foraging parties, and on the 4th the Earl warned the Committee of Both Kingdoms that he expected to be attacked from both sides. Supplies were short, "the country rising unanimously against us", and he hoped to secure Lostwithiel until enough provisions could be sent in from Plymouth or elsewhere to enable him to move. By 11 August the Parliamentarian army was boxed in around Lostwithiel. Grenvile had secured Bodmin, and the line of Royalist outposts ran from Grampound up to Bodmin, to Boconnoc and on to Liskeard.

The Committee was well aware of Essex's plight long before this letter reached London. Parliament had already voted that £20,000 should be sent to Plymouth to provide pay and provisions for his army, and ordered Waller's lieutenant-general, Sir John Middleton, to march to Essex's aid with 2,000 horse and dragoons: detachments from Parliamentarian garrisons in the south-west were to join him as he marched. Another £10,000 was voted for Waller's army, but by 27 August Waller had got no further than Farnham. Essex remained more confident that events warranted, hoping that a relief force would reach him, and unaware that contrary winds would prevent the fleet from arriving. Nevertheless, it is to his credit that he refused two offers to surrender, the first, made by the King, offering him "eminent marks of his confidence and value".

The Royalists were not without their own difficulties. The upper echelons of court and army had long been riven by factionalism. Lord Wilmot, lieutenant-general of the horse, was heartily disliked by Prince Rupert. Clarendon described him as "proud and ambitious, and incapable of being contented...he drank hard, and had a great power over all who did so, which was a great people".[2] In pride and vanity, Wilmot had been making seditious remarks, and his rival George Digby, a protege of Rupert's, took care that these were reported to the King. On 8 August Wilmot, mounted at the head of his troops, was arrested for high treason by the knight marshall, and sent under escort to Exeter. George, Lord Goring, who had recently arrived with the army, was appointed in his place, and Hopton relieved Lord Percy, the less than efficient General of the Ordnance. Although Wilmot had been popular, Goring was well enough accepted in his place, and the replacement of Percy by Hopton could do nothing but good.[3]

iii. The Battle of Lostwithiel

The bare bones of Essex's deployment were sound enough, given the position in which his army now found itself. Restormel Castle, north of Lostwithiel, was a roofless shell, but its strong walls and commanding position made it a natural outpost. Colonel John Weare's Devonshire Regiment garrisoned the castle, and it was prepared for defence long enough for an embrasure to be opened in the upper wall of the chapel to enable a light gun to sweep part of the castle's high mound.[4] Further bodies of foot were posted on the hills on either side of the town, with particular emphasis on Beacon Hill, just south of the main Liskeard road. There is, however, no evidence that field fortifications were thrown up on Beacon Hill or the other high ground surrounding Lostwithiel, an omission for which Essex deserves criticism.

The town itself was firmly held, for its Tudor bridge was the most southerly point where the River Fowey could be crossed dryshod. Another strong detachment of foot

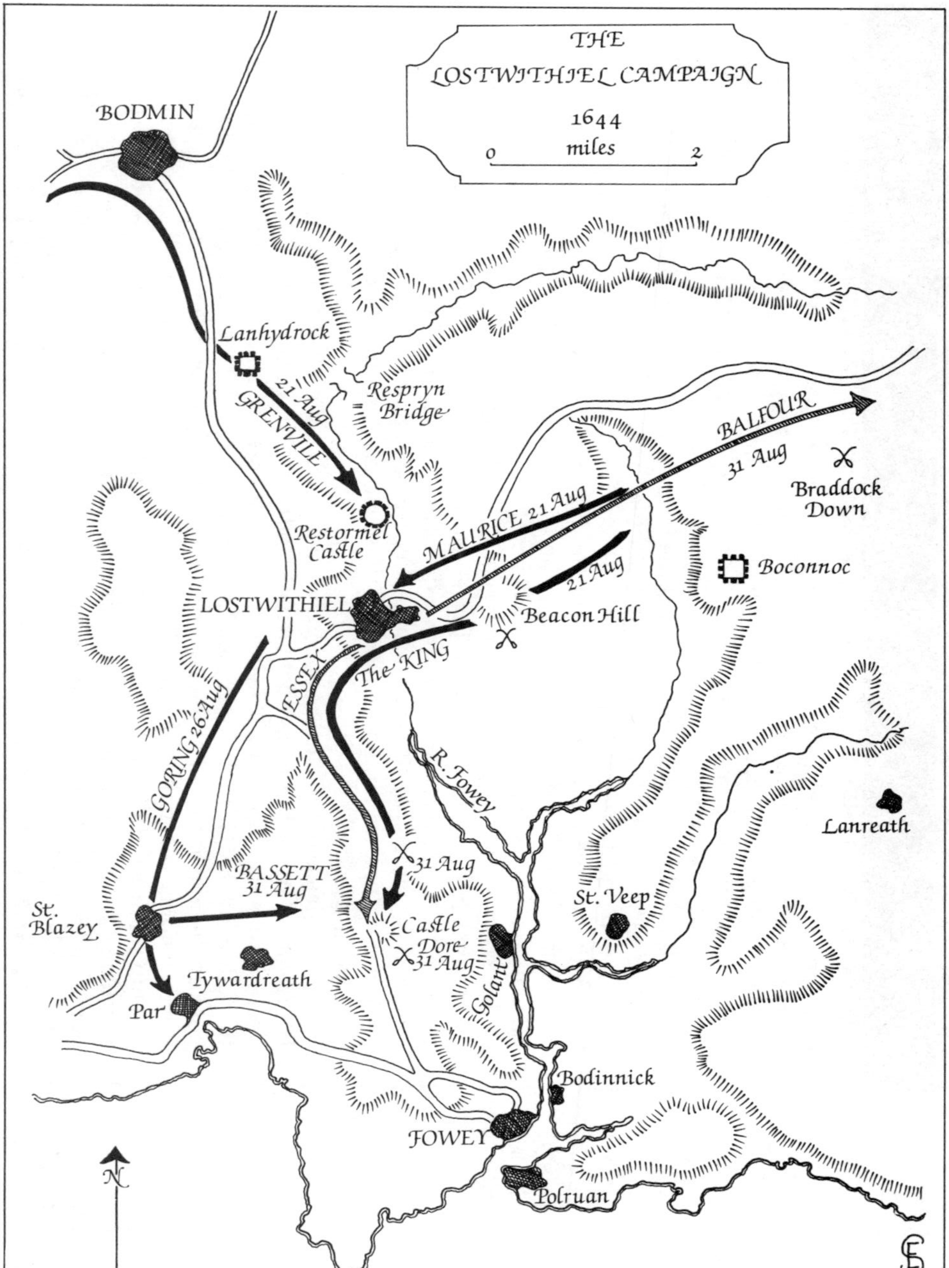
THE
LOSTWITHIEL CAMPAIGN
1644
miles
0
2
BODMIN
Lanhydrock
21 Aug
GRENVILE
Respryn
Bridge
Restormel
Castle
LOSTWITHIEL
MAURICE 21 Aug
BALFOUR
31 Aug
Braddock
Down
Boconnoc
21 Aug
Beacon Hill
The KING
ESSEX
GORING 26 Aug
R. Fowey
Lanreath
31 Aug
BASSETT
31 Aug
St. Veep
St.
Blazey
Castle
Dore
31 Aug
Golant
Tywardreath
Par
Bodinnick
FOWEY
Polruan
N

garrisoned Fowey. Essex's cavalry were posted in Lostwithiel itself—the Royalist Richard Symonds, serving in Lord Bernard Stuart's troop of horse, complained that they held a mock ceremony in St Bartholomew's Church, christening a horse Charles "in contempt of his Sacred Majesty"—and patrols were no doubt used to keep open communications with Fowey.

Sir William Balfour, who commanded the horse, was a capable Scots professional who had served in the Dutch and Scottish armies, and had enjoyed Royal favour as lieutenant of the Tower of London in the 1630s. It was probably his intense dislike of popery that drew him towards the Parliamentary opposition, and he refused to connive at the Earl of Strafford's escape, proving immune to bribery. He fought well at Edgehill, and had a hand in Waller's victory at Cheriton. The foot's Major-General Philip Skippon, a veteran of the Dutch service, had commanded the London Trained Bands—easily the most effective of the country's militia forces—at the outbreak of war, and was one of the steadiest infantry officers on either side. Clarendon complained that he was "altogether illiterate", but acknowledged that he was "a man of good order and sobriety, and untainted with any of those vices which the officers of that army were excercised in".[5]

The first phase of the battle opened when Grenvile, with 2,400 men, secured Respryn Bridge on 11 August, the day that he took Bodmin. This enabled the Royalists to operate on both sides of the Fowey even though Essex still held Lostwithiel bridge. On the following day Grenvile occupied Lanhydrock itself, further tightening the Royalist hold on the northern end of the battlefield. Essex's plight worsened on 13 August: Royalist horse seized the ford over Penpoll Creek at St Veep, occupied another of Lord Mohun's houses, Hall, by the Bodinnick Ferry, and took the lightly defended fort at Polruan. Two hundred foot with two or three guns were posted in the fort, which commanded the entrance to Fowey harbour. Colonel Sir Charles Lloyd's regiment was quartered in Cliff, across the Fowey from Golant, to cover the ferry there.

In the week that followed the Royalists carried out reconnaissances and made plans:

Charles was viewing the southern end of the Parliamentarian position from the walk below Hall House when he was fired on from across the river, and a fisherman standing near him was killed. News arrived of Middleton's relieving force: it had got as far as Bridgwater, only to be beaten by Sir Francis Doddington, and had retreated on Sherborne. The weather remained too bad to permit Warwick's fleet to intervene: in any case, the loss of Polruan fort meant that Essex was now restricted to the tiny port of Par or the coves at Menabilly and Polkerris.

At 7.00 on the misty morning of 21 August the Royalists began a general advance east of the Fowey. Grenvile took Restormel Castle after a weak resistance. Colonel Weare, a veteran of Stratton, had the unhappy knack of being in the wrong place at the wrong time, and blamed the mishap on the fact that unsolicited reinforcements, sent by Essex, had departed precipitately. In any event Grenvile secured not only the castle but an adjacent ford over the river. Further south, the Royalists took the high ground east of Lostwithiel, including Beacon Hill, which dominates the town. With Beacon Hill secured, Maurice sent a column 1,000 strong to take the high ground north of the Liskeard road. That night the Royalists threw up a redoubt twenty yards square on Beacon Hill: at dawn the next day the freshly turned-earth looked, to the Parliamentarians below, like a body of closely-ranked horse.

There was sporadic fighting over the next few days, and guns in the "King's Redoubt" on Beacon Hill bombarded the town, damaging the church. Essex's guns replied, but to little effect. This is hardly surprising, for it is a little over a mile from the redoubt to Lostwithiel church. The Royalist guns, firing downhill at a large target, would not have found the task beyond them, but Essex's demi-culverins, trying to hit an earthern rampart a mile away and 400 feet above them would have been at the outer edge of their effectiveness.

The bombardment so reduced movement in the town that the King's council of war suspected that Essex was falling back to Fowey. Another general advance was planned for the 25th, and half the cavalry was sent across Respryn Bridge to reinforce Grenvile.

When it became clear that the Parliamentarians were still firmly established in Lostwithiel, the advance was cancelled. The Royalists had time on their side. Supplies reached them regularly—on 26 August convoys came in from Dartmouth and Pendennis, with 1,000 barrels of powder. Essex, in contrast, was running short of food, and on the 26th the King sent Goring with 2,000 horse and Major General Sir Thomas Bassett with 1,000 foot around the Parliamentarian lines to St Blazey, to prevent the Earl's men from foraging in that direction and to secure the port of Par. Nevertheless, the result of the campaign was not pre-ordained. Essex still had 10,000 men, and if their morale was blunted by persistent reverses and atrocious weather—it was an unseasonably wet August—a force that size, with officers like Balfour and Skippon at its head, could not be treated lightly. The King had about 17,000 men at his disposal, but they were deployed along a fifteen mile front, at the mercy of bad communications.

On the evening of 30 August two deserters were brought to the King's headquarters at Boconnoc. They revealed that Essex intended to retire to the coast with his infantry and guns that night: Balfour was to break out with the cavalry. The King reacted promptly. Warnings were sent to Goring at St Blazey, and to the detachments at St Veep and Polruan, while a courier spurred off to Colonel Sir William Waldegrave at Saltash, ordering him to break down the bridges over the Tamar. The entire army was to stand to its arms that night, and fifty musketeers were posted in a house on the Lostwithiel-Liskeard road. The Lifeguard of Horse, quartered at Lanreath, received the warning at about 1.00 am on the 31st, and rode to Boconnoc.

Despite these precautions, the Parliamentarian cavalry escaped. It was a dark and foggy night, though this cannot excuse the fact that at about 3.00am Balfour's column passed the fifty musketeers without being engaged. Lord Cleveland managed to get about 250 horse together, but this was too small a force to stop Balfour, and it was not until dawn that Cleveland, now with 500 men, was able to pursue the Parliamentarians over Braddock Down and Caradon Down. Balfour shrugged off an attack by Waldegrave in Saltash, managed to ferry his men across the river, and reached

Plymouth with the loss of only about 100 soldiers. It was a fine performance, and an index of what resolute leadership could achieve even in inauspicious circumstances.

The Royalists were exasperated by the episode. Clarendon blames Goring for it, alleging that he was in one of his jovial excesses when the order to pursue reached him. It is, however, hard to see quite what Goring, at St Blazey with the bulk of his cavalry, could have done about a breakout to the east. Moreover, Sir Edward Walker, who, as secretary of the council of war had access to high-level discussions, acknowledges that Goring only received the first warning at 10.00am on the 30th, and was not ordered to pursue until late that afternoon.[6] The reason for Royalist failure to intercept Balfour was less a case of simple incompetence (though the musketeers' commander cannot have had a pleasant interview with his colonel) than the problems inherent in holding a long cordon of poor communications. And although the army had been ordered to stand to, it is clear that many Royalists were widely dispersed in search of provisions, and that in the King's army of 1644 giving an order was one thing —ensuring that it was executed was quite another. We must consider what might have happened had Essex left guns and baggage in Lostwithiel, and sent his foot out with the horse. It is likely that they too would have broken clear, for it would have taken the Royalists several hours to have organised any cohesive pursuit. The one advantage Essex enjoyed was that of having his force concentrated under his hand—but he did not use it.

The King set off in pursuit of Essex's main body shortly after dawn. The Parliamentarians had a small number of Royalist prisoners who were kept in the belfry of St Bartholomew's Church, and the prisoners pulled up the ladder and declined to come down. Their captors tried to dislodge them with musket fire and smoke. When this failed, they exploded a barrel of gunpowder which lifted the roof, whose original line can still be seen on the wall of the tower. An attempt was also made to destroy the bridge, but the demolition party was visible to the Royalists on Beacon Hill, and at about 7.00am 1,000 foot advanced into the town and drove them off with their task unfinished. Two or three guns were at once brought up and positioned in the old Parliamentarian lines in Lostwithiel to engage the rearguard on the hill to its west, and the pursuit began in earnest.

The Parliamentarians moved off down the narrow road to Fowey, their guns and a small body of infantry rearguard, characteristically commanded by Skippon, bringing up the rear. Essex's account is much-quoted but deserves reiteration for the unique view it provides of that wet and dispiriting morning:

> The ways were so extreme foul with excessive rain, and the harness for the draught horses so rotten as that in the marching off we lost three demi-culverins and a brass piece, and yet the Major General fought in the rear all day, he being loth to lose these pieces, thirty horses were put to each of them, but could not move them, the night was so foul and the soldiers so tired that they were hardly to be kept to their colours.[7]

The King, at the head of his Lifeguard, forded the river south of Lostwithiel at 8.00am, using a ford shown him by an officer named Stephens, who was a local man. As a reward, he took a silver cup from his saddle-wallet and gave it to Stevens: it is still in the hands of a local family, and Canon Miles Brown describes it as "a plain goblet about six inches tall and three in diameter at the top".[8] As the King's detachment cut across the Parliamentarian line of withdrawal, it soon found abundant evidence of a disorderly retreat, including a cartload of muskets and five cannon abandoned in the mud.

The Royalists, led by Grenvile's Cornish foot and the King's party, pushed the Parliamentarians back, hedge by hedge, until their resistance thickened on the shoulder of high ground between Tywardreath and the Fowey at Golant. Between 11.00 and 12.00am Grenvile's men fell back as the Parliamentarians stood their ground, but rallied on the King's Lifeguard of Foot under Lieutenant Colonel William Leighton. The Lifeguard of Horse at once charged the Parliamentarian infantry, driving them from some of the hedges they held despite a hot fire. Major Brett, who had led the

Queen's troop to the attack and carried on despite being shot in the arm at the first hedge, was riding back to have his wound dressed and was knighted on the spot, the King using the drawn sword in his hand to dub him Sir Edward Brett.

The main body of the Royalist foot came up at about 2.00pm, and Colonel Matthew Appleyard took its vanguard straight into action against the hedges, thickly garnished with Parliamentarian musketeers. At the same time Major-General Bassett, marching up from St Blazey, fell onto the Parliamentarian left flank. Yet there was still some life left in Essex's army. Captain Reynolds, with three troops of horse which had not accompanied Balfour, counter-attacked, well supported by Essex's own regiment of foot, and drove the Royalists back across several fields, but withdrew as the Lifeguard approached. Goring rode up at 4.00pm, was ordered to set off after Balfour, and at once did so. Another counter-attack boiled up at about 6.00pm, but the arrival of the Earl of Northampton's brigade of cavalry helped turn it back.

The hill-fort of Castle Dore, its double entrenchment commanding the countryside around, dates from the second century BC, and in the fifth century AD is believed to have housed the great hall of King Mark of Cornwall. By early evening on 31 August it formed the centre of the Parliamentarian defensive line, with Essex's artillery in position on its ramparts. To the west of Castle Dore stood Essex's own regiment and Colonel Butler's musketeers, while Weare's, Barlett's and Robartes' regiments held the ground to the east of the entrenchments. The Parliamentarians had too few men to hold a solid line from the Fowey to the coast, and so the flanks of the Castle Dore position must inevitably have been turned. In the event, however, Weare's regiment disintegrated at nightfall, dragging back adjacent units, and the utter defeat of Essex's army was only a matter of hours away.

The Earl himself could not bear to await the end. He had left the conduct of the retreat to Skippon, and when the latter sent messengers to ask for orders on the night of 31 August-1 September he received only the helpful suggestion that he should try to bring the army to Menabilly and Polkerris. Failing that, he should use the threat of blowing up the train of artillery to secure the best possible surrender terms. Then, accompanied by Sir John Merrick and Lord Robartes, Essex slipped away to Plymouth in a fishing boat after dawn on the 1st. "I thought it fit to look to myself," he explained, "it being a greater terror to me to be a slave to their contempts than a thousand deaths".[9] Skippon, slightly wounded but as resolute as ever, presided over a council of war later that morning. He argued that the foot should try to break out as the horse had done: even if they failed, he concluded, "it is better to die with faithfulness than to live dishonourable".[10] These sentiments did not appeal to his officers, who knew that their men were at their last gasp, and the council decided to ask for terms. Officers and soldiers above the rank of corporal were to retain their arms; able-bodied soldiers would be escorted to safety, and the sick and wounded would be looked after at Fowey until vessels could take them to Plymouth. These terms were in part a tribute to the personal courage of Skippon, but were also a reflection of the fact that the Royalist army was itself running short of supplies.

The agreement was concluded on 2 September, and that afternoon the Parliamentarians set off in the pelting rain. Symonds thought them "so dirty and dejected as was rare to see, none of them except some few of their officers did look any of us in the face".[11] The King's army behaved badly towards its prisoners, and there was much taunting and not a little looting, despite the energetic attempts of Charles and his officers to stop it. The country people were far worse: many Parliamentarians were robbed of the very clothes they stood up in. Of the 6,000 soldiers who had surrendered, perhaps as few as 1,000, by Sir Edward Walker's pessimistic reckoning, lived to see their homes again: the rest died of hunger, disease and exposure along the way. The savage treatment of Essex's men was, in some measure, a reflection of the destruction they themselves had caused. Jonathan Rashleigh's fine house at Menabilly had nothing but bare walls left, while in Lostwithiel the Parliamentarians had vandalised the Great Hall and destroyed the Exchequer Records stored there.

The surrender crowned a resounding victory. Amongst its more material benefits were 42 guns, a mortar, 100 barrels of powder and 5,000 arms. Charles knighted the sheriff, Francis Bassett, declaring: "Now, Mr Sheriff, I leave Cornwall to you safe and sound." He then marched from Boconnoc to Liskeard, and thence to Plymouth, which had recently received Lord Robartes as its governor. Charles summoned Plymouth on 11 September, but when it refused to open its gates he left Grenvile to blockade it and marched on to Tavistock and thence to Chard, Sherbourne and Salisbury, leaving garrisons behind him as he went. He hoped to relieve Banbury Castle, Basing House and Donnington Castle before returning to Oxford. He had been reinforced by Prince Rupert, but his enemies grew stonger by the day. Waller fell back ahead of him, joining the Earl of Manchester's army at Basingstoke on 18 October. The indomitable Skippon brought the survivors of Essex's foot up from Portsmouth to meet them, and Balfour's horse had already rendezvoused. With such a substantial force in his way, the King could not hope to reach Basing House, but he marched on to Newbury and relieved Donnington Castle.

On 27 October the united Parliamentarian army attacked the Royalists just north of Newbury. While Manchester menaced the right front of the Royalist position, Waller led an outflanking column right around it and vigorously assailed the Royalist left, held by Maurice with the Cornish horse and foot. Eight hundred of Essex's musketeers spearheaded the attack, eager to avenge themselves on the Cornish. They broke into a redoubt held by Maurice's men, clapping their felt hats over the touch-holes of the guns to prevent them from being fired: these were some of Essex's guns from Lostwithiel, recaptured by the very men who had lost them.

Despite this local success, the Parliamentarians had failed to bring their superiority to bear, and the Royalists were able to draw off safely. After much manoeuvring, the King managed to slip a provision convoy into Basing House, and went into winter quarters around Oxford in November with his short-term objectives achieved. The disputes in the Parliamentarian council of war before and after Newbury were echoed in impassioned argument in London, testifying to growing dissatisfaction with the conduct of the war. This led to the passage of the Self-Denying Ordinance, which excluded all members of both houses of Parliament from military command, and the formation of a single force with unified command. From the powder-smoke wreathing 1644 emerged the war's decisive instrument: the New Model Army.

5. THE END IN THE WEST, 1645-46

i. New Modelling

Early 1645 was dominated by the raising of the New Model Army. Although it had originally been intended that the New Model should replace all Parliament's other armies, some local forces remained, and it took longer than expected to fill the New Model's ranks. Raising the cavalry presented few problems, but though existing armies furnished most of the infantry, men had to be pressed into service in London and the Home Counties, and the army took the field in May 4,000 men short. Its general, Sir Thomas Fairfax, had fought the Spanish in the Low Countries in 1629-31 and commanded a troop of horse in the Bishops' War. Although beaten at Seacroft Moor and Adwalton Moor in 1643, he helped win in the victories at Winceby and Marston Moor and, being neither peer nor MP, was a natural choice for command. His lieutenant-general, Oliver Cromwell, was a Huntingdonshire gentleman, MP for Cambridge in the Long Parliament, totally without military experience until he raised a troop of horse in 1642. He established himself as a cavalry leader of tactical flair and firm decision, and was, exceptionally, given a commission in the New Model despite his seat in the Commons. Fairfax was allowed to appoint his own officers, and in this respect he had a notable advantage over predecessors and opponents alike.

The Royalist army was also reorganised, though on nothing like the same scale. In November 1644 Charles decided to replace his general, Patrick Ruthven, Lord Forth, a loyal but tired and bibulous veteran, by Prince Rupert. Rupert was anxious not to be seen as commander-in-chief, and so the fourteen-year-old Prince Charles was appointed generalissimo, with Rupert as de facto "supreme commander of the Royal armies under the King".[1] Clarendon, as ever hostile to Rupert and his faction, lamented the removal of Forth, and was no happier with Goring's promotion to command the horse in Rupert's place.[2]

In February 1645 peace negotiations, the Treaty of Uxbridge, failed, and active operations resumed. Goring had been busy in the south-west, where he narrowly failed to take Weymouth and advanced to Farnham before falling back into Dorset.

Plymouth held out against Grenvile, and he and Goring were soon at daggers drawn. Goring proposed an attack on Taunton by his own army and Grenvile's force, aided by Sir John Berkeley, governor of Exeter, but by the time Grenvile had received firm orders to co-operate the opportunity had passed.

The King had long planned to give Prince Charles a measure of genuine responsibility, and in March the Prince was sent down to the West as commander-in-chief. He took with him an advisory body of Privy Councillors, including Sir Edward Hyde, later Earl of Clarendon, whose writings are one of the major sources for the war. The Prince also received advice from the council which administered the Duchy of Cornwall on his behalf. Such an arrangement was bound to cause difficulties, and squabbling amongst Royalist commanders in the West made matters no easier. When Charles left Oxford for Bristol, it was discovered that no arrangements had been made to maintain his court or escort: as Mary Coate observed, it was "an ignominious opening of the campaign in the west, and typical of the want of cooperation between the central and local authorities which characterised it".[3]

The Prince's arrival did little to end the bickering. A new army was to be raised to take Taunton, and although Hopton, a member of the Prince's council, had the best claim to command it, Grenvile obtained the post. Berkeley took over the siege of Plymouth, and Goring was mollified by having extra foot raised for his army. Friction in the West mirrored disputes at the centre. Rupert's long list of enemies grew, and both the Queen and the Marquis of Newcastle, in France, did their best to discredit him. Royalist fortunes teetered in the balance in Wales and Cheshire. Bringing troops over from Ireland had added new bitterness to the struggle, and Parliament declared that the "Irish" should be hanged if captured. East Anglia and the south-east were firmly in the hands of Parliament, and the North was lost after Marston Moor. Only in Scotland did the horizon seem bright: the Marquis of Montrose, the King's lieutenant-general there, trounced the Covenanters at Inverlochy in February, and told the King: "I doubt not before the end of this summer I shall be able to come to your Majesty's assistance with a brave army".[4]

The news from Scotland helped give Charles an optimistic view of the situation not shared by others. Rupert favoured a concentration on Worcester, followed by a march to relieve Chester, the raising of troops in Lancashire and Yorkshire, and perhaps a march further north to join Montrose. Some of the King's most capable advisers were with Prince Charles, and at Oxford Rupert's inveterate enemy Digby ensured that the decision to send the artillery to join Rupert for a campaign in the North was delayed. It was delayed too long, for in April, Cromwell took a brigade of horse to Oxford, captured an outpost and destroyed a body of foot marching in from Wales, while the remainder of the New Model prepared to march to the relief at Taunton.

The King's council of war met at Stow-on-the-Wold on 8 May. Rupert championed his Chester scheme, maintaining that if the city fell it would be impossible to land reinforcements from Ireland. The remainder of the council favoured marching West, but Rupert feared that no good could come from the brawling generals there. It was decided that Goring should return to the West to face Fairfax, while the remainder of the army moved North.[5]

Fairfax was ordered to Taunton on 28 April, and reached Blandford on 7 May. Then the Committee of Both Kingdoms, hearing that Rupert had turned northwards, directed Fairfax to push a brigade on to Taunton but to swing back towards Oxford with the rest of his army. He at once detached Colonel Weldon, who reached Taunton just in time. The Royalists had entered the town: Colonel Blake's garrison had taken refuge in the castle, and but for Weldon's approach would have been overwhelmed.

Fairfax had moved quickly to Oxford, surrounding it in late May. News of Rupert's storming of Leicester on 31 May, however, prompted the Committee of Both Kingdoms to order Fairfax to break up the siege and set off to find the King and Rupert. And find them he did. On 14 June the New Model fought its first major battle just north of the little Northamptonshire village of Naseby. It was a stunning victory. About 1,000 Royalists were killed and more than 4,000 taken, and though the King escaped, he left behind him all his cannon, and much damaging correspondence which was published as *The King's Cabinet Opened*.

Goring was again battering Taunton when Naseby was fought. not long after the meeting at Stow there had been another change of plan, and he had been ordered to take his army North to join the King, but he had declined to do so, supported by the Prince's council, which maintained that its position would be impossible without Goring's force. This left the Royalists open to defeat in detail, for Naseby was no forgone conclusion, and Goring's men might have made all the difference. After the battle, while the remnants of the King's army hovered on the borders of Wales, Fairfax again moved West. Despite the rapidity of the New Model's advance—it averaged seventeen miles a day for five days in blazing weather—squabbling amongst the King's generals continued, and the ill-discipline of Royalist troops induced many Somerset men to form bands of Clubmen to resist their depredations.

Goring, outnumbered two to one, fell back before the New Model. He failed to hold the line of the Yeo, but successfully deceived Fairfax into sending part of his army in pursuit of a small detachment. This availed him nothing, for on 10 July Fairfax routed his army at Langport, pushing it into a disorderly retreat. Bridgwater fell on 23 July, and smaller garrisons were snapped up. Fairfax then swung north-east, and on 4 September he summoned Bristol, held by Rupert himself. When the New Model attacked on the 11th it quickly broke into the defences, and Rupert surrendered on terms. His exasperated uncle dismissed him from his command and ordered him abroad. Charles himself set off for Chester, only to see his horse cut to pieces on Rowton Heath on 24 September, and eventually made his way back to Oxford. Elswhere his garrisons crumbled. Cromwell took Devizes on 23 September and Winchester early the next month. Basing House, so long a thorn in the Parliamentarian side, was carried by assault on the 14th. The news from Scotland was equally depressing: Montrose's little army had been destroyed at Philiphaugh.

ii. Fairfax in Cornwall

The strain of a long war, exacerbated by the feuding amongst Royalist dignitaries, sapped Cornish resolve. Grenvile and Goring remained at loggerheads, and while Goring lay at Tiverton, in the path of the coming storm, Grenvile sought, with almost manic energy, to call together the Cornish *posse comitatus*, haul in deserters and punish disloyalty. Only the exhaustion of the New Model saved Exeter, and at last Goring, pleading illness, retired to France. Lord Wentworth replaced him, but promptly declined to receive orders save from the Prince himself. Cromwell surprised his horse in winter quarters at Bovey Tracey, and Wentworth retreated into Cornwall: the siege of Plymouth was raised for the last time, and amidst bitter recriminations, the Royalists crossed the Tamar.

On 15 January 1645 the Prince's council offered the command to the only available general with an unblemished reputation: Lord Hopton. It is an index of Hopton's motto—"I will strive to serve my Sovereign King"—that he accepted. Wentworth was to command the horse and Grenvile the foot, but on 18 January Sir Richard formally refused to obey Hopton: he was arrested and sent under guard to St Michael's Mount. The arrest of Grenvile further demoralised the Cornish. An astonished Hyde wrote that even those who had complained most about his depredations resented his arrest. There was a particularly Cornish quality to loyalty which outsiders found it hard to grasp.

Fairfax did not stay in winter quarters for long. Despite heavy snow, he took Dartmouth on 18 January, capturing 1,000 men and 120 guns. The Cornishmen in the garrison were sent home with two shillings in their pockets and the Lord General's assurance that he came to save their county, not ruin it. This was a marked change from the plundering ways of Grenvile's men, and it encouraged the arrival of Devonshire recruits and the surrender of Powderham Castle. Exeter proved more obdurate. Although his position was desperate, Berkeley refused to surrender, and Fairfax eventually decided to leave a force to mask the city, and set off to meet

Hopton. Fairfax was influenced by the news that the Queen and Lord Jermyn had obtained permission to raise troops in France, but intelligence of the dispute between Hopton and Grenvile was even more telling.

Hopton advanced from Stratton to Torrington, taking with him cattle to reprovision Exeter. A Parliamentarian source credits him with 5,000 horse and 4,000 foot, but Hopton admitted to only 3,300 horse and 1,890 foot. His cavalry were worse than useless—Clarendon called them "horse whom only their friends feared and their enemies laughed at, being only terrible in plunder and resolute in running away".[6] On 14 February Hopton heard that Fairfax had moved up from Crediton to Chumleigh, and began to prepare Torrington for defence, barricading the roads and posting his foot about the town, sending some of his horse to reconnoitre, and using the remainder to flank the barricades, with a dragoon detachment posted at Stevenstone Park, a mile outside the town.

Fairfax advanced from Ring Ash on the 16th, and that afternoon he drove in the dragoon picket from Stevenstone. By nightfall he was in contact with the Royalist infantry, and decided to wait till dawn before assaulting. Soon, suspicion that Hopton would withdraw under cover of darkness encouraged him to push on, and at 9.00pm he attacked. Hopton complained that his men quickly fell back from the barricades, but Fairfax, in his letter to Speaker Lenthall, wrote of how: "The dispute continued long at push of pike and with butt-ends of muskets".[7] A Parliamentarian soldier who fought there acknowledged: "They maintained the barricades, lines and hedges, with as much resolution as could be expected, and had not our men gone on with extraordinary courage, they would have been repulsed".[8] Forced from the barricades, the Royalist foot streamed out of the town, and there was chaos as Cleveland's horse attempted to re-enter it. At this juncture the Royalist powder, stored in the church, blew up—probably by accident—killing 200 Royalist prisoners and some Parliamentarians, with a sheet of roof-lead narrowly missing Fairfax himself. Hopton, a horse killed under him and his face gashed by a pike, fought his way out with the rearguard, but the battle cost him 60 killed and 600 prisoners: it was the end of his foot.

   Hopton considered breaking away with the horse to join the King, but decided that they would not face Cromwell's men in the open, and fell back to Stratton. Fairfax marched on into Cornwall, brushing Hopton's horse from the Tamar crossings at Stratton on 24 February to reach Launceston on the 25th and Bodmin on 2 March. He took care to secure the bridges as he advanced, to prevent the Royalists from breaking back past him, and he sent Hugh Peters, zealous chaplain to the train of artillery, to use his influence—he was himself a Cornishman—to dissuade the inhabitants of the eastern part of the county from rising in the New Model's rear.

   Hopton fell back with the tatters of his army. Most of his officers advised him to surrender, but he refused to do so without the consent of the Prince, and sent a messenger off to Pendennis to obtain this. Prince Charles was no longer there. News of Fairfax's advance had persuaded his council to advise him to seek safety in the Scilly Islands, and the royal party had left on 2 March. In the meantime, Hugh Peters arrived in Bodmin with commissioners appointed to negotiate the surrender of Mount Edgecumbe. Fairfax used the opportunity to distribute news, found in letters taken in a ship at Padstow, that 6,000 Irish were awaiting transport to England and 4,000 more would follow shortly. Peters announced the imminence of the Irish invasion at a general meeting at Bodmin on 6 March, further depressing Royalist standing in the county.

   Fairfax offered Hopton terms: officers and men were to be free to go abroad if they chose, troopers who handed in horse and arms would receive twenty shillings apiece, and Fairfax would use his good offices with Parliament on Hopton's behalf. While he was waiting for an answer, Fairfax beat up Royalist quarters at St Columb, and, as Hopton played for time, advanced to Tregony. At midnight on 9 March Hopton at last admitted that the game was up, and asked for terms, naming Tresillian Bridge, just east of Truro, as the rendezvous. Terms were agreed on 12 March, and the surrender took place on the 15th. On the 16th Lieutenant Bonython offered to surrender St Mawes Castle, and across the county the disbandment of the residue of the King's last army went on.

There was one important exception. Shortly before his surrender, Hopton had sent reinforcements to St Michael's Mount and Pendennis Castle. Pendennis was under the command of Colonel John Arundell of Trerice, known as "Jack for the King" or "Old Tilbury." With him were a number of diehard Royalists—a Parliamentarian pamphleteer called them "desperate persons"—including Colonel Walter Slingsby, and the supplies sent into the castle in March made a long siege possible. Pendennis was blockaded on 17 March, and on the 18th Fairfax went to view the castle, accepting as he did so the surrender of Dennis Fort on the Helford estuary. Arundell, however, sent the firmest of rejections to Fairfax's summons[9]
Fairfax left the castle blockaded by a force under Colonel Robert Hammond, and went off to deal with unfinished business elsewhere.

Exeter surrendered to Fairfax on 13 April, and St Michael's Mount, held at much personal expense by Sir Francis Bassett and, after his death, by his brother Sir Arthur, promptly did likewise. Oxford itself fell on 24 June and Worcester a month later: although Harlech Castle still held for the King, Pendennis was his only other remaining mainland garrison. Arundell remained obdurate. He declined a summons from Hammond and another from Vice-Admiral Batten, although the besiegers threw a line of entrenchments across the neck of the peninsula on which the castle stands, with a redoubt in its centre and batteries elsewhere, and bombarded the castle from the land while Batten in the *St Andrews* blockaded it by sea. Arundell had plenty of ammunition, but shortage of food soon caused concern, and a ship sent in by Hyde was taken on 7 June. At the end of the month Arundell and his senior officers sent a desperate appeal to the Prince, who they believed to be in Jersey, but it took some time to reach him because he had departed for France. There was in any event little that he or his advisers could do to help.

Further defence became impossible in early August. There was sickness in the garrison, and many men deserted. On the 15th Arundell at last agreed to negotiate with Batten and Colonel Richard Fortescue, who had replaced Hammond, now governor of Exeter. It was typical of his temper that he signed the surrender document "condescended unto by me John Arundell," and only a mutiny by the men prevented some of the wilder officers from blowing up the magazine. Such of the garrison as could still stand marched out with the honours of war—drums beating, colours flying, musketeers with bullets in their mouths and matches burning at both ends. Some returned home and a few sailed for France. Amongst them was Sir Henry Killigrew, mortally wounded by a splinter from a shot he had fired after the surrender had been agreed. He had attempted to burn down his house, Arwenack Manor, on the peninsula jutting down to Pendennis, to prevent the Parliamentarians from using it: he was a fine example of the tough Cornish gentry who had championed the King's cause with such exemplary courage.

EPILOGUE

i. Keeping the Peace

The King hoped to play the Scots off against their allies, and on 5 May 1646 he rode into the Scottish lines at Newark. In January 1647 the Scots handed him over to Parliament, and he was soon secured by the New Model. For the rest of the year he busied himself in negotiations with the Scots, and eventually agreed to impose Presbyterianism on England in return for Scottish military support. This "Engagement" was the direct cause of the Second Civil War, and outrage at the King's behaviour pushed the Independents, the dominant group in Parliament, towards the conclusion that the King must die.

From 1646 until 1660 Parliament's County Committee was supreme in Cornwall. It is a measure of the far from revolutionary character of the Civil War that it was dominated by landed gentry: as Mary Coate observed, "the Royalist was ruled by his equals, who preserved intact the Tudor tradition of unpaid service to the State".[10] The Committee collected taxes: no easy task, for the county was impoverished and there was widespread hostility to Parliament. It also oversaw, in conjunction with London-based and local committees, the sequestration of Royalist estates, and the process of compounding whereby "delinquents" were allowed their estates back on payment of a fine. Some of those who had surrendered to Fairfax had favourable treatment included in their terms: others were able to persuade the Lord General to intercede on their behalf. More suffered severely for their loyalty, with expensive litigation capped by huge fines: Jonathan Rashleigh, whose house had been ruined by Essex's soldiers, was heavily fined into the bargain. The sale of land by impoverished families led to a redistribution of property, although the men who obtained the land were, in general, already from the landowning class themselves. Thus Colonel John St Aubyn, a prominent local gentleman and Parliamentarian officer, bought St Michael's Mount from the heir of Sir Francis Bassett in 1657.

The Second Civil War, which broke out in February 1648, saw revolt in Wales and parts of the south-east combined with invasion by the Scots. Cromwell dealt decisively with the invasion, defeating it at Preston, while Fairfax subdued the south-east and went in to take the Royalist stronghold of Colchester. There was a rising at Helston, the "Gear Rout" which ended in a scrambling little battle on an ancient earthwork near St Mawgan, and other smaller stirrings. The only significant Royalist success was the recovery of the Scilly Islands, which remained in Sir John Grenvile's hands till 1651. Some Cornish MPs were ousted in Pride's Purge in December 1648, while, at the other political extreme, three sat on the High Court of Justice which condemned Charles I to death in January 1649.

The execution of the King encouraged Hopton, now commanding a small fleet based on the Scilly islands, to issue a declaration to the inhabitants of Cornwall, and in 1649-50 Royalist privateers, assisted by sympathisers on land, were a major danger to shipping off the coasts of Cornwall. In February 1649 Charles II was proclaimed in Scotland, and another Scottish army was raised for the invasion of England. Risings were planned to coincide with this, and Hopton, lieutenant-general of the King's forces in the West, called for support, but the county was watched too closely. Charles and the Scots were defeated at Worcester in September, and this disaster ended the war. Parliament took the Scilly Islands in May 1651, and treatment of Cornish Royalists became more stringent.

The plotting went on. As former supporters of Parliament were alienated by politcal and religious developments, notably by Cromwell's assumption of the title of Lord Protector in December 1653, so disaffection spread, with prominent Presbyterians aligning themselves with the Royalists. By 1654 even Lord Robartes was a secret supporter of the "Sealed Knot", a covert Royalist organization warmly championed by Sir John Grenvile, Sir John Arundell of Lanherne, John Arundell of Trerice and John Trelawney. In March 1655 small bands of Royalists rose in Yorkshire, Northumberland and Nottinghamshire, and Colonel John Penruddock and Sir Joseph Wagstaffe enjoyed a brief spree in Wiltshire and Somerset before Desborough's troopers hunted them down. There were arrests in Cornwall, and Royalists were further fined to pay for a militia established in every county to maintain order. In October the country was divided into ten regions, each headed by a major-general: John Desborough, Cromwell's brother-in-law, kept a keen eye on the Western counties.

John Grenvile and Jonathan Trelawney were lucky to escape arrest when a fresh Royalist plot was discovered in 1658. Grenvile was in trouble again the following year, but continued to work actively for a restoration of the monarchy, using Nicholas Monck, nominated to the family living in Kilkhampton in 1653, as an intermediary in his negotiations with General George Monck, an increasingly powerful figure following the death of Cromwell in September 1658. Cornwall proved as resistant to government pressure in the 1660 elections as it had in their pre-war counterparts, and several prominent local Royalists were elected. It was a fitting tribute to the sacrifices made by the Grenviles that Sir John Grenvile presented to the Commons the King's letters offering a settlement: the House responded by sending commissioners to negotiate with him.

ii. Rewards and Legacies

Charles II rewarded many of his supporters handsomely. Grenvile became Earl of Bath, Viscount Grenvile of Lansdown, Baron Grenvile of Bideford and Kilkhampton, and Lord Warden of the Stannaries. "Jack for the King" Arundell did not live to see the Restoration, but died in straightened circumstances in 1656. His son's elevation to the peerage in 1664 was a just reward for the family's loyalty. Sir John Berkeley became Baron Berkeley of Stratton, but the real author of that victory was past recompense: Ralph Hopton had died in exile in Bruges. Richard Grenvile, too, died abroad, but it is entirely in character that his gravestone was reputedly engraved "The King's General in the West". Robartes was better remembered for his late support than his early opposition, and in 1679 he became Earl of Radnor and Viscount Bodmin. Yet there were limits to royal generosity. A wholesale reversal of the land redistribution was out of the question, though the Duchy of Cornwall was re-established and its lands re-possessed or leased back to their purchasers. St Aubyn remained secure on St Michael's Mount—his successors are there still—and although Sir Richard Vyvyan, Master of the Exeter Mint during the war, became Governor of St Mawes and a Gentleman of the King's Privy Chamber, he remained massively out of pocket.

The King was merciful to most of his opponents, but there was no hope for those who had tried Charles I and signed his death warrant. Of the three Cornishmen who had done so, William Say escaped abroad, but John Carew and Gregory Clement were both executed. So too was Hugh Peters. Although he had not signed the warrant, he was exempted from the general Act of Indemnity.

The wounds inflicted by the war on the Cornish landscape are long since healed, though some of their scars remain. The battlefield of Braddock Down lies on private land, and is too thickly wooded for the landscape to whisper much of its history to the visitor. Stratton has more to say. The eminence of Stamford Hill, still wooded on its eastern flank, dominates the surrounding countryside, and sufficient roads and footpaths lace it for the visitor to be able to trace events. A monument, erected by the Grenviles, stands on the western edge of the earthwork in the centre of Stamford's position. The Ordnance Survey map places its crossed swords marking the site of the battle a little to the west of this spot: the curious visitor should look just east of the little road across the hill, just beyond the aptly-named Bevil House. The Wall of the old Manor House, now the Tree Inn, bears a commemorative plaque, and there are some relics of the battle in the church.

The King's campaign about Lostwithiel has left abundant evidence. St Nectan's chapel, between Lostwithiel and Boconnoc, lost its tower in the fighting, and still retains only a stumpy appendage. Between the chapel and the town Beacon Hill swells out just south of the Liskeard road. Traces of the redoubt are on private land, hidden by the brambles covering old mine workings, but this undergrowth, on an otherwise bare hill, is visible from the main road and from the town below, and shows just how commanding the redoubt was. The Tudor bridge still spans the Fowey in Lostwithiel, and the fine church of St Bartholmew is nearby. Traces of the damage inflicted by the explosion of the barrel of gunpowder can still be seen, as can the octagonal font of Pentewan stone, used in the mock christening which so outraged Richard Symonds.

North of Lostwithiel stands the Norman shell keep of Restormel Castle, once owned by Richard Earl of Cornwall and subsequently Duchy property. It is now administered by English Heritage. At the top of the outer wall of the roofless chapel is an embrasure commanding the ditch and countryside to the north, probably inserted when John Weare's men held the castle. To the north-east stands Respryn Bridge, in an idyllic setting at the foot of the park around Lanhydrock. It is not hard to think of Goring's troopers clattering over the bridge in 1644. After the war Lord Robartes planted a great avenue of sycamores, now largely replaced by beeches, leading from Respryn Bridge to the house. A fire in 1881 destroyed almost all of Robartes' house, leaving only the north wing and entrance porch standing: it was, however, rebuilt to the same plan and is now in the hands of the National Trust.

The ground between Lostwithiel and Castle Dore, with its pattern of fields broken by stout hedges, is much as 17th Century accounts describe it, and Castle Dore nudges the little road from Fowey to Lostwithiel. Across the Fowey from Golant is Cliff, and a cottage there has two cannon balls above one of its windows, fired by Parliamentarian gunners from across the river in a vain attempt to clear Sir Charles Lloyd's men from the crossing site. Further South, but also on the east bank of the river, is Hall, now a farm, and near it runs Hall Walk, where Charles was narrowly missed by a shot in 1644. Polruan fort still sits squarely at the entrance to Fowey harbour, grinning at the defences opposite.

On his way to Truro from Lostwithiel the traveller crosses Tresillian Bridge, scene of Hopton's surrender in 1646, a fact commemorated on a plaque on one of the houses at its eastern end. Pendennis Castle is the jewel in the crown of Civil War Cornwall. like many fortresses elsewhere it displays layers of defences, from Tudor masonry to the concrete of the 20th Century. Its keep has been sensitively furnished by English Heritage, and the upper gun deck bears replicas of the cannon once mounted there. The outer ramparts, with their geometrical regard for flanking fire, are in a good state of preservation. The elegant outer gateway, through which the visitor enters the castle, was finished about thirty years before the Civil War, and in low season, when the place is quiet, you may be forgiven for hearing the tuck of drum as old Jack Arundell leads his emaciated garrison out of the fortress.

St James' church at Kilkhampton, north of Stratton, bears the imprint of the Grenviles. In the family chapel the arms of John, 1st Earl of Bath, stand above the screen, a tablet commemorates Sir Bevil, and a stained glass window pays tribute to the martial Grenviles. The Grenvile houses at Stowe—the old house that Bevil and Richard grew up in, and the splendid new mansion built by John—have vanished. The farmhouse of Stowe Barton stands on their site, but the walls and terraces of John's garden remain. Across them blows the keen wind from the Atlantic, pummelling the Cornish coast today as it did when Bevil took his tenantry out to Stratton behind the griffin banner. Battles are won and lost, great families rise and fall, but the land endures.

NOTES

Chapter 1
1 A. L. Rowse **Tudor Cornwall** (London 1949) p.14.
2 Charles Thomas **Tintagel Castle** (London 1986) p.11.
3 Quoted in Rowse **Tudor Cornwall** p.117.
4 Ibid p.217
5 Quoted in C. H. Firth **Cromwell's Army** (London 1962) p.3.
6 Rowse **Tudor Cornwall** pp.388-9.
7 Here I dissent slightly from Firth **Cromwell's Army** pp.60-61.
8 See William Eldred **The Gunner's Glasse** (London 1646) and Brigadier O. F. G. Hogg **English Artillery 1326-1716** (London 1963).
9 An important exception is Martin van Creveld **Supplying War: Logistics from Wallenstein to Patton** (London 1978).
10 Quoted in Firth **Cromwell's Army** p.209.
11 Mary Coate **Cornwall in the Great Civil War and Interregnum 1642-60** (Truro 1963) p. 1. This is a work of fundamental importance, upon which I have relied heavily, although Miss Coate and I sometimes differ in matters of military detail.
12 Perez Zagorin **The Court and the Country** (London 1969) pp.117-8.

Chaper 2
1 The Vindication of Richard Atkyns (Ed Brigadier Peter Young, London 1967) p.12.
2 Sir Ralph Hopton **Bellum Civile: Hopton's Narrative of His Campaign in the West (1642-1644) and Other Papers** (Ed C. E. H. Chadwyck-Healey, Somerset Record Society, 1902) p.47.
3 Ibid p.25.
4 Ibid p.27.
5 Ibid p.28.
6 J. Simmonds "The Civil War in the West" in A. L. Rowse (Ed) **The Civil War in English History** (London 1949) p.86.
7 Sir Thomas Wrothe to John Pym, 20 January 1643 **Historical Manuscripts Commission, Portland Manuscripts**, Vol I p.92.
8 Sir Bevil Grenvile to Lady Grenvile, 19 January 1643, quoted in Coate **Civil War** p.43.
9 Hopton **Bellum Civile** p.33, Sir Bevil Grenvile to Lady Grenvile 9 February 1643 quoted in Coate **Civil War** p.47.
10 The London Bookseller George Thomason collected contemporary pamphlets, news-sheets and so on over the period 1640-1661. These are henceforth listed as TT with the appropriate reference number. For conflicting accounts of the Launceston battle see "A Full Relation of the Great Defeat given to the Cornish Cavaliers by Sergeant Major Chudleigh", 2 May 1643, TT E.100.20, and "A True Relation of the Proceedings

of the Cornish Forces under the command of the Lord Mohun and Sir Ralph Hopton", May 1643, TT E.102.17. See Also Hopton **Bellum Civile** pp.36-7.
11 Hopton **Bellum Civile** p.42.
12 For accounts of Stratton see Hopton **Bellum Civile** pp.41-2 and "The Truth of our bad News from Exeter', 20 May 1643, TT E.103.12. Coate cites an enthusiastic letter from Sir Francis Bassett to his wife, from the privately-owned Bassett Manuscripts, and the diary of Colonel Robert Bennett of Hexworthy, also privately owned. Chudleigh's conversion is explained in "A Declaration..." TT E.37.20, and Stamford's charges appear in "A Perfect Diurnal" TT E.249.12.

Chapter 3
1 Coate **Civil War** p.100.

Chapter 4
1 Edward Hyde, Earl of Clarendon **History of the Rebellion...** (8 Vols, Oxford 1826), I p.202.
2 Ibid IV p.526.
3 Wilmot never came to trial. After spending some weeks in confinement, he was released to go abroad. There was probably nothing more than foolishness and vanity behind his "Sedition."
4 C. Raleigh Radford **Restormel Castle** (London 1986) p.11.
5 Clarendon **Rebellion** II p.105.
6 Sir Edward Walker **Historical Discourses upon Several Occasions** (London 1705) p.75
7 John Rushworth **Historical Collections** (8 Vols, London 1721) V p.702.
8 H. Miles Brown **Battles Royal: Charles I and the Civil War in Cornwall and the West** (Lostwithiel 1982) p. 59. I am most grateful to Mrs. Hilda Chanter of Lostwithiel for drawing this book to my attention and, indeed, for lending me her own copy of it.
9 Rushworth **Historical Collections** V p.703. For discussion of the Earl's decision see Bulstrode Whitelocke **Memorials of the English Affairs** (London 1682) p.98, and a supportive "Attestation of the Officers of the Army..." in Rushworth **Historical Collections** V pp.708-9. Weare, tried for alleged failure at Restormel and Castle Dore, justified himself in "The Apologie of Colonel John Weare..." TT E.21.34. He was briefly imprisoned but subsequently re-employed.
10 Ibid p.704.
11 Richard Symonds **Diary of the Marches of the Royal Army during the Great Civil War** (Ed C. E. Long, Camden Society 1859).

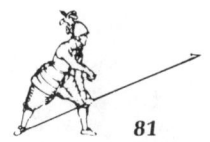

Chapter 5
1 Patrick Morragh **Prince Rupert of the Rhine** (London 1976) p.121.
2 Clarendon **Rebellion** V pp.1-2.
3 Coate **Civil War** pp.168-9.
4 Quoted in C. V. Wedgwood **The King's War** (London 1966) p.392.
5 Clarendon wrote that the arrangement suited both Rupert and Goring: Rupert would not have to contend with the influential Goring, and Goring would have a free hand in the West. The suggestion reflects Clarendon's antipathy for both noblemen.
6 Clarendon **Rebellion** V p.306
7 Rushworth **Historical Collections** VI p.101. For Hopton's account see his "Relation of the Proceedings in the West of England" in Thomas Carte **A Collection of Original Letters and Papers..."** (2 Vols, London 1739), I p.109. Fairfax's chaplain, Joshua Sprigge, produced a useful if uncritical account of the New Model's operations on **Anglia Rediviva** (London 1647): for Torrington see pp.192-202
8 Quoted in Coate **Civil War** p.203.
9 R. Scrope and T. Monkhouse (Eds) **Clarendon State Papers** (3 Vols, London 1767-86) II p.228.